TIME OF ARRIVAL

TIME OF ARRIVAL

and

Other Essays

Dan Jacobson

———◆———

THE MACMILLAN COMPANY
NEW YORK

32,015

To

Adolf, Aaron and Bunny

in friendship

Acknowledgements

Most of the essays in this book were first published in *Commentary* (New York) and *Encounter* (London). I would like to thank the present editors of these magazines, Mr Norman Podhoretz and Messrs Melvin Lasky and Stephen Spender, as well as their predecessors, for the hospitality they have offered me in their columns. My sincere thanks are due also to Mr Karl Miller, formerly of the *Spectator* and now of the *New Statesman*, for the encouragement and help I have had from him. In addition, I am glad to make acknowledgements to the editors of the *Nation* and the *Noble Savage* in the United States, and the *Jewish Chronicle* in England.

D. J.

Contents

CONTENTS

Part One

ENGLAND

A*

TIME OF ARRIVAL

I

IT WAS JUST AFTER midday that the boat docked at Dover;
and we went through the Customs shed and on to the pallid
grey platform of the railway station. With all the anxieties
of arrival upon me, in England for the first time, a few days
after my twenty-first birthday, I nevertheless felt at peace.
One could not help feeling at peace, the station was so quiet,
the officials were so homely in appearance, the voices of the
passengers were raised in such a clear, almost bird-like way. I
bought *The Times* and the *New Statesman*, and felt with gratification, after years of handling only the overseas editions, the
thickness of the paper between my fingers; and saw with the
same gratification that the dateline on the papers was the
actual date, not that of two or three weeks before. So I was in
England, truly in England at last. I had not known how much
I had wanted to be in England until then; until, on that platform, an anxiety came to rest, and something else within me—
an ambition perhaps, or a hope—began to stir.

I remember vividly those casual yet oddly decisive moments
on Dover station, and the very different moment of arrival at
Victoria; but nothing of the journey between. Victoria seemed
huge to me, echoing, dark; and the black-clothed people
scurried about bewilderingly under the vault, in all directions.
Fortunately, I was travelling with my brother, who had been
in London before, and knew his way about the city a little.
As it was still early in the afternoon we decided we would not
bother for the moment about finding accommodation, but

would simply leave our luggage in the station cloakroom and go out for a look around.

The pavements outside were a little paler than the overcast sky; the cobbled space in front of the station seemed overcrowded with lumbering red buses. We did not go far on that first exploration; we merely caught one of the buses to Hyde Park Corner, crossed into the park, and walked up towards Marble Arch. Already, on that walk, I was struck by what was for me to be one of London's most surprising features: its spaciousness, the size of its streets, squares and public places. (The size of the city itself was another matter, and quite distinct from what I am speaking of here: in a way, the area the city as a whole covered did not come as such a surprise to me, partly because I could not, and still cannot, grasp it: it is beyond reckoning, beyond the widest span of one's imagination.) I suppose I had heard so much about the 'tight little island', about England being 'cramped', 'crowded', and 'pinched'— and had also heard so much about the 'wide open spaces' of South Africa, about the 'vastness' of the veld—that somehow in my mind there was an expectation that everything in England would really be small, reduced in scale, somehow toylike. And it was true that many of the individual buildings were small, and did seem to have been rammed against one another, in a frozen jostle for space. Nevertheless, again and again, on other walks, I was to be surprised by such random things as the sheer mass of the piers and arches of bridges; the width of the steps leading up to monuments; the height of the trees in the parks, and the expanses of grass around them; the acres upon acres of the city given over to railways gleaming in parallel lines; the stretches of terraced houses which seemed to wear their encrusted ornamentation like a frown, and which stood in endless repetition down wide, windblown streets.

On that first walk it was Hyde Park itself which was imposing, and the lumps of statuary just inside and outside the park, and the glimpses of streets and buildings beyond. It was midafternoon, in late March, and bitterly cold; there seemed to be nothing spring-like in the air, though I was surprised to see how green was the grass in the park. From nowhere, it seemed, a gust of rain was suddenly dashed into our faces as we walked;

it did not seem at all to have come from the sky. The gust
ceased as abruptly as it had begun. But the sun did not come
out; it looked as though the sun never had come out, and never
would. And through the streets, between the trees, over the
grass, the light *moved*. That is the only way I can describe the
thickness of the light; the swiftness with which it changed; the
slightness of the individual changes; the way it could change at
a distance and yet remain unchanged near by. It was as if
between ourselves and the source of light there had been put an
infinite number of filters, out of which one or two or several were
being lifted, to be replaced only when others nearer or farther
from ourselves were removed, in a perpetual alternation.

Within this shifting light, colours had a strange intensity;
they seemed to well up within each object in a continual
process, instead of being a static, hard, settled dye or tone.
And because of this suffusion, this seepage, of colour, one
almost expected the objects themselves to be vague in outline,
to run together; and so their precision and firmness of line
came invariably as a surprise. This was true even of the faces
of people, which were either vague or suddenly vivid, featureless or disconcertingly quick in expression. And even on that
first walk I saw how fine, how subtle, how eccentric the faces
of the English were. Each face seemed to carry within it the
shadows, the suggestions, of innumerable others which had
neither come to the surface nor been entirely lost.

Unexpectedly, it began to grow dark, really dark, though it
was not yet five o'clock. So we had to think of finding an
hotel; and went back from Marble Arch to Victoria. My
brother knew that there were many cheap hotels in Bloomsbury,
and we told a taxi-driver simply to take us there. He drove to
Tavistock Square, and we stopped at the first hotel we saw. It
was a narrow converted house, and everything inside it was
narrow too: the entrance-hall, the manager's cubicle, the
manager's face, the staircases, the room into which we were
eventually shown. The room smelled heavily of damp; it had a
single large window, overlooking a fire-escape and a brick wall;
right against the sky, above everything else, a battery of
chimney-pots stood poised. An Irish maid came in to make up
the beds; an elderly woman with eyes that seemed to move

about too much, under a tired, deeply lined brow. She was silent throughout, until my brother went out of the room; then she came up to me, took my arm with her hand in a fierce grip, brought her face close to mine and said passionately, 'You're lucky there's the two of you. It gets too queer when you're alone!' A moment later she was gone.

Quite by chance I had been reading on my way to England a miscellany which contained, among other things, a collection of letters written by Virginia Woolf to Logan Pearsall Smith. The letters had been addressed, I remembered, from Tavistock Square; and I got the book from my suitcase and looked up the number of the house she had lived in. When we came out of the hotel we walked around the square, looking for the house among the black, flat dwellings on two sides of the square. But the house no longer existed. We leaned over a low brick wall, looking into a hole in the ground. Down below were stumps of walls, some of them overgrown, others showing bits of coloured plaster and tile. Great wooden beams rose out of the hole to buttress the building from which the one on this site had been severed.

I must have spent hours, during my first few weeks in London, looking into the bomb sites, wondering about them, searching in myself and never finding a response which seemed to me adequate. Many of the ruins were dramatic, even melodramatic, to look at, with bare flat walls like shadows, and the sky showing through gaps which had once been doors and windows; others were merely quiet, waste, charred spaces, with only a few ledges and bits of brick to show the basements of what had once been houses, churches, office-blocks, blocks of flats. How could such weights of masonry have been brought down by flame and explosion into heaps of rubble? And how had the rubble been carted away, leaving the streets trim, though gaping? In the end one had to look at the ruins as one looked at everything else: as part of the spectacle of London, as another sign of the things that people had done over the hundreds of years they had been in London, just another evidence of their having lived and died in the place.

Anyway, the house Virginia Woolf had written from was no

longer there, and I was disappointed to see this. But the rest of
the square was presumably much as it had been when she had
been alive and had written her letters to Logan Pearsall Smith.
He and Virginia Woolf had exchanged elaborate, self-conscious
mock-insults about 'Chelsea', which he was supposed to
represent, and 'Bloomsbury', which of course was hers. And
what they had meant by Bloomsbury I saw to be these trees,
houses, the glimpses of the university buildings, the traffic in
Southampton Row. Was there nothing else? And within the
disappointment that the house should have been scooped out of
the square another began to grow. So this was it. I had seen it.
True, I had not seen, and was unlikely ever to see, any of the
people who had made up the Bloomsbury society; but the
physical Bloomsbury was about me. And the disappointment I
felt was not with its appearance, which was black, severe and
imposing enough, but arose simply from my having seen it. I
would never be able again to make up a Bloomsbury of my own
imagination—a district cleaner, perhaps, or brighter, less hard
and angular, filled with happier people. I would not have
exchanged my glimpse of the real Bloomsbury for anything I
might have been able to imagine; but still, there was a loss.

And another loss I knew was my own imagination of myself
in Bloomsbury, or anywhere else in London. Coming to London
had not—not yet, at any rate—changed me, transformed me,
made a new man of me. Bloomsbury was what it had been
before I had seen it. So was I.

Breakfasts in the hotel were gloomy meals, taken in a small
dining-room where everybody spoke in subdued tones, but for
one man in a checked suit who rustled his *Daily Telegraph*
loudly and demanded almost every morning, in a stentorian
voice, that they give the 'cat' to the 'hooligans' whose doings he
read about in the papers. He was strong on niggers too. He was
like a caricature of the hanging, flogging Englishman of the
worst kind: seething with grievances and rages which red-
dened his round face, thickened his voice, and made his small
blond moustache bristle. He was my first living exemplar of the
English flair for self-imitation; the zeal, the wholeheartedness
with which many Englishmen conform to certain ideal types of

such familiarity, not to say staleness, that the outsider positively
expects some 'real' man buried within the type to give him a
secret wink of irony, a little gesture or nod of complicity. But
the outsider waits in vain. The man (or woman) is absorbed
completely in his role. Don or dustman, *New Statesman* intellectual or flogging Tory, debutante or char: it is impossible to say
which came first, the type or the individual. So it was with this
man; and so too, in a different way, it was with the other guests
in the hotel, who appeared to be either students or a few
elderly ladies who lived there permanently. (There were no
foreigners among them, apart from ourselves.) None of the
other guests ever argued with or even commented upon the
remarks of the hanger and flogger. Instead, in a curious, dismal,
admirable English way they managed wordlessly to dissociate
themselves from him without putting forward any views of
their own. Indeed, still wordlessly, they even managed to
suggest that it wasn't so much the man's views they disapproved
of, as the vehemence with which he put them forward. The
hotel, incidentally, unlike others in the neighbourhood, did
not have a single African or Indian guest.

Breakfast was the only meal we took in the hotel: most of the
time, by day and in the evenings too, we were out sightseeing.
We went to Westminster Abbey; we wandered about the Strand
and St Paul's and the City: we stood in Piccadilly and Parlia-
ment Square; we went to Downing Street and across St James's
Park and into Mayfair. And did I actually see the streets and
buildings in front of me, as we went about, or was I merely
remembering the pictures I had seen of them, the descriptions
I had read of them? It was impossible to say. It was impossible,
in those first confused few weeks, really to look at the buildings.
All I could do was to confirm that they were there, as the
pictures and books had told me they would be. There was deep
satisfaction in this confirmation: so deep I cannot easily
describe it, for it was not just the reality of the buildings that
was confirmed, but also, in an odd, unexpected way, my own
reality too.

So place ran into place into place in a progression that
seemed endless in length and breadth, and was limited in other
dimensions only by my own ignorance. At every point the

progression yielded some interest; it could not help doing so, for the pleasure of confirmation did not wait upon the famous buildings or vistas, but could be roused by any ordinary street or sign, both for what it was and for being where it was. However, one great fact about London was so overwhelming that I couldn't possibly think of it as a recollection or a reminder of what I had already been told; and that fact was the shabbiness of the city.

I think I would have found London shabby under any circumstances, because of the sky above it: everything, I felt, must look its worst under a sky that continually trailed clouds and smoke low over the buildings, and sometimes thinned a little to reveal a sun coloured like the blood-spot in an egg. But I had come to London a few years after a war which had halted the erection of new buildings, and the repair of old ones, which had destroyed or partially destroyed thousands of others; and which had then left the country to endure a kind of siege of rationing, austerity, and gloom. There were times, often, when I felt that an inward dissolution would do as effectively over a wider area what the bombs had done where they had fallen; and that the blackened, gutted hulks of houses one saw everywhere were the condition towards which the whole city was slowly, inevitably sinking, of its own momentum. The public buildings were filthy, pitted with shrapnel-scars, running with pigeon dung from every coign and eave; eminent statesmen and dead kings of stone looked out upon the world with soot-blackened faces, like coons in a grotesque carnival; bus tickets and torn newspapers blew down the streets or lay in white heaps in the parks; cats bred in the bomb-sites, where people flung old shoes, tin cans, and yet more newspapers; whole suburbs of private houses were peeling, cracking, crazing, their windows unwashed, their steps unswept, their gardens untended; innumerable little cafes reeked of chips frying in stale fat; in the streets that descended the slope from Bloomsbury to King's Cross old men with beards and old women in canvas shoes wandered about, talking to themselves and warding off imaginary enemies with ragged arms. And as for the rest of the people—how pale they were, what dark clothes they wore, what black homes they came from, how many of them there were swarming in the streets, queueing on the pavements, standing packed on underground escalators. You saw crowds when you left the hotel, you travelled a mile and saw crowds, another mile and more crowds, another mile the same; and around them always the same rundown, decaying, decrepit, sagging, rotten city.

One night I walked about in an area which I now suspect must have been Paddington, on my way to an address I have forgotten and so cannot return to. I remember crossing a bridge over some railway lines, and looking across the parapet to a desolation of railway lines, shunting and stationary trains, red and green winking lights, floodlights on tall towers, iron and brick sheds from which flames occasionally broke. It was early evening, but the sun had been gone for hours, if it had ever shown itself at all during the day, and white smoke rose in plumes from the railyard and drifted across and between the lights. It seemed as though a town, a whole country, lay beneath me; and the bridge I stood on spanned it all. Farther along, on the other side of the bridge, was a terrace, with a little private road running the length of the row. The houses were four or five storeys tall, and were in darkness; each had its portico in front of it, with gaunt fluted pillars holding it up. Even in the half-light one could see how dilapidated they all were; ruined, cavernous, peeling. I knocked on the door and no one answered; I had come to the wrong place. But I did not move away immediately. Standing on that abandoned doorstep, with the hoarse sound of the railyard in my ears and the darkness of the portico over me, I knew that I wanted to be lost, lonely, anonymous; I wanted to feel within myself the dissolution of all that I had been before by name and background.

Yet, confusingly, this city offered me a continuity between past and present, between words and things, which I had hardly known I was seeking until it was offered to me. And past and present pointed to the future. How could I avoid dreaming of the friends I might make in London, the fame I might win there, the houses I might one day be able to enter?

I had the addresses of just two people in London, neither of whom was a friend of mine, and with whom I was unable, as it turned out, to establish any kind of friendship. I had hoped that these people would help me to find a room; but in the end I found one simply by catching a train to the Finchley Road Tube Station, and then walking up the road until I came to one of those glassed-in little notice-boards, advertising rooms-to-let and 'light removals' and vacancies for charwomen. (I went to Finchley Road because my brother had advised me to try the Hampstead area; he had never been out to Hampstead, but had heard that it was a pleasant area to live in.) Many of the notices for rooms carried discouraging messages like 'Gentiles Only' or 'British and Gentile Only' or 'No Coloureds' or even, testifying to some obscure convulsion of the English conscience, 'Regret No Coloureds'. I went to the nearest address which seemed as though it might be prepared to take me, in a street that ran directly off the Finchley Road. The house was a three-storeyed Victorian giant of a place; the housekeeper lived in the basement, a school of dancing occupied the ground floor, and the rest of it was let in single and double rooms.

The housekeeper was a woman with dyed blonde hair, and a mouth painted in the shape of a Cupid's bow, even though her upper lip did not in the least have a suitable shape for one. So the bow was simply drawn on, heavily, the peak of it coming just under her nose, where a man might have worn a moustache, and the tips of it reaching into her cheeks on both sides. She looked drunken, clown-like, in that paint, and I never saw her without it. But I never saw her drunk either. In fact, she was a quiet, artless woman who slept with one of the lodgers on the top floor, and perhaps for that reason was not given to prying into the affairs of the others in the house. And she kept the place clean. The room I was offered was small, sparsely furnished, and fitted with the inevitable, ancient gas-fire and gas-ring. But the view out of the window was a wide one: one looked over the Ministry of Food offices in the Finchley Road to the vague dark spread of South Hampstead, Kilburn, Willesden, Paddington, places whose names I did not even know.

I took my luggage into the room, and then I went to see off my brother at Waterloo Station. Once he was gone, I had

absolutely nothing to do. I decided I would go into Regent's
Park, which I had been in before, and had liked. But previously
I had entered the park from Baker Street; this time I got off
the train at Regent's Park Station, and found myself in a park
that looked nothing like the one I was slightly familiar with.
Flat green plains of grass stretched away to black trees on the
horizon; there was hardly a soul about, for it was mid-morning
on a weekday. I began walking across the park; the silence
and emptiness of it made me feel nervous; even the pallor of my
shadow on the grass was strange. Eventually in the distance I
saw what looked like the crumbling battlements of a castle—
there seemed to be a central circular keep, and crenellated
walls going down on both sides of it. It looked ruinous, historic,
ominous, lifted up against the horizon. It was the zoo, I found
out, when I came closer. The thought of going in to stare at the
animals seemed even more desperate than the thought of going
back to my room. I continued walking, pretty much in a circle
—I had no alternative really, in Regent's Park—and at last
came out at Baker Street. From there I did what I had been
funking since I had left my brother: I went back to my room.

The house was quiet; it was only in the afternoon that the
dancing-classes began, when the piano jangled and the floors
shook with the combined thumping of all the little girls who
came to the house carrying their dancing shoes in small cloth
bags. I looked out of the window, over the glitter of the traffic
in the Finchley Road, towards the vague blue and black
spread which was only a part of the city, and which yet stretched
to the very limit of my sight. I had come to London. London
did not care.

Shortly after I had moved into my room, a friend in South
Africa wrote that I should look up G.; I would get on well
with him, my friend promised me. This, I found out, was
true enough: it would have been true of practically anybody,
for G. was indiscriminately affable and garrulous. He was a
slight, stoop-shouldered man in his middle twenties, who
appeared much older than he was, chiefly because of the
prominence of his pale, bald, soft-looking scalp. G. was living
with a Cockney woman, an ex-prostitute (or so G. claimed),

whose previous lover was in jail, from where he wrote letters describing how he was going to 'cut up' G. when he got out. G. told me all this within a few minutes of our meeting. He told me about it not only because he was garrulous, but because he was very proud of his girl-friend, her criminal admirer, and his own association with them both—all of it was so far from the Johannesburg Jewish respectability in which he had been brought up. He lived in a basement-flat in Belsize Park: an ill-lit subterranean place with huge rooms, rubbish-bins at its entrance, and Picasso prints on its walls. Gas-fires and electric lights seemed always to be burning in the flat, and the smell of damp was driven out at intervals only by the smell of bacon and eggs.

Maisie (or was her name Milly?) listened complacently to G.'s account of their situation; she was slight and fair-haired, and seemed demure enough, until she spoke. When she spoke, she swore: at the weather, at a pot she might be trying to clean, at the landlord, at G. He used to call Maisie 'my love' and 'my sweetheart', exaggeratedly, on every possible occasion; but no endearment ever crossed her lips. G. had a theory, I remember, that a man who thinks a thought or visualises a scene is as much an artist as the man who writes down his thought or puts the scene on canvas; and no matter what we used to begin talking about, we would sooner or later find ourselves discussing this theory. He himself was writing a novel which would, he said, demonstrate the theory: when I asked him why, in view of the nature of the theory, he bothered to *write* the novel, he answered with several other theories which I have altogether forgotten. But quite another answer was given by Maisie: 'Him! Write a book? That'll be the f——ing day!'

Through G. I met Naomi K. and her husband. Like G., Naomi was South African, Jewish, and from a well-to-do home; and like G. again, she was in flight from all these things. She was married to a tall, bearded, and more-than-faintly anti-Semitic Gentile, who used to torment her by imitating her parents' accents. ('Dey vanted Naomi to marry a nize bizhnezh boy,' he would say, charmingly.) Both Naomi and he were painters, and they lived off what she earned as a teacher in the nursery-department of a small orthodox Jewish school. Naomi was a tiny, jumpy, black-haired woman, who was continually expressing girl-like enthusiasms over cats, or dogs, or children, or budding trees. Derek, her husband, was enthusiastic about nothing, except perhaps about puncturing Naomi's enthusiasms, which he did with an air of great fatigue, made all the more disdainful by the smoke that dribbled from his lips when he spoke. She would falter and apologize; he would dribble more smoke. On the whole it was much more painful to be with them than with G. and Maisie.

These were my only friends in London at that time. I feel guilty in writing disparagingly of them now—just as I used to feel guilty, then, in visiting them. I felt guilty because I knew that I would hardly have sought their company if I had had other people to visit. But I simply knew nobody else. I used solemnly to ration myself to seeing each couple on alternate Sundays only, I remember. At their flats, on these odd Sundays, I met a few other people—most of them South Africans, a few of them Americans or Australians—but I became friendly with none among them. In all, the first months of my stay in London were as lonely as any I have ever experienced. Even after I had got a job as a teacher at a small private school I was as lonely as I had been before, after school-hours and on weekends.

But I must say that at first I felt my loneliness to be really disturbing or frightening only when it was brought home to me as something else—as a kind of inward dislodgement or displacement of my own senses. There were two recurring and almost hallucinatory experiences which had this effect on me. Sometimes, in the crowded streets I used to see approaching me a man or woman whom I had known in Johannesburg. I would feel no especial surprise at this, until, as I drew nearer, the resemblance between the person approaching and my acquaintance would suddenly and totally disappear. Then I would realize that I had felt no surprise at 'seeing' X or Y or Z because I had imagined myself to be *in* Johannesburg. The shock was always a double one: I was shocked that I should have fallen into the fantasy, and I was shocked on coming out of it to see around me once again the streets of a colder, darker and infinitely bigger city. The other experience was very similar, and usually occurred when I came out of a cinema or theatre. Being disorientated, I would look around to find the way I should go, and a few times I found myself walking perhaps half a block under the impression that in this direction lay the Melville tram terminus, or Eloff Street, or Park Station—all of which are in Johannesburg, not London. And a further complication of these experiences was the fact that Johannesburg was not my home-town; merely the other big city in which I had once lived, and in which I had at times been lonely too.

It was one thing, I realized, to be lonely; another to be lost. And it seemed that I could submit more easily to the first than to the second. I was all the more grateful, therefore, that almost all of London, though new to me, was yet familiar in a ghostly way; and that the familiarity should have been so sustaining, even exhilarating. I have said that much of London was a 'recollection' or a 'reminder' of what I had been told to expect; but what I felt is better described by saying that everywhere I went I saw the visible, external frame or setting of much that had hitherto seemed to exist only within me, and that I had never truly believed could exist in any other way. Now I saw the sky under which so many imagined actions had taken place, and the streets where they had been enacted: these were the faces the protagonists had worn and these the accents in which they had spoken. It was as though the sponge of my imagination had been dry before; but now, immersed in the English medium, it slowly filled itself and expanded. The medium was thicker and heavier than I could ever have anticipated; ultimately it was more burdensome too. There was so much I did not know and never would know; there was so little I could ever do, in comparison with what had been done and done and done and done a hundred thousand times, and more. Yet better that burden, I was sure, than none at all.

In the Charing Cross Road, one night, I saw the performance of an escape-artist and his assistant. By the time I joined the crowd, the artist had already been completely covered in a kind of canvas shroud, which the assistant was knotting with ropes in front and behind. The assistant was stripped to the waist, the artist was a bundle without face or limbs, and the

arena on which they performed was marked out on the pavement by a long leather whip which the audience was not
supposed to cross: the show was deliberately intended to appear
obscene and sadistic. The assistant pitched the bundle on to
the ground, and then chained it up, jocularly pushing it about,
hectoring it, tugging hard at the ropes and chains, and eventually leaving it lying on the pavement while he went around
demanding money from the crowd. The skin of his shoulders
was goosepimpled with cold. On the pavement the bundle
breathed, but was otherwise quite still. When the collection
was over, the assistant picked up the whip, trailed it over the
ground, and suddenly lifted it as to strike at the creature under
him. But he just cracked the whip in the air, once, and a
second time, and the bundle began writhing and squirming,
its chains rattling and tinkling against the cement slabs, grunts
and heavy breathing coming from within it. It rolled over and
over, towards the audience and back again; occasionally it lay
still before contracting and expanding in a spasm.

The man succeeded in freeing himself in the end: a wizened,
gingerish face peered morosely out of the shroud, and the
audience immediately began to disperse, as if everyone in it was
ashamed of himself. There was no applause, and the man
obviously expected none. He had escaped too many times
before; and had seen too many crowds edge guiltily away from
him.

Summer came: or rather, summer slowly diffused itself. The
weather was not hot, merely warm, but the warmth was like
heat in comparison with the cold that had persisted for so
long before. I remember looking out of the window of my
classroom, one afternoon, while the boys were busy with their
exercise books, and being surprised at the sight of the sun
shining directly upon the street outside: I had never before
seen it so strong and clear, in England. Yet behind its rays
there was still a blue or grey vibration in the light, a hint of
darkness. And on another afternoon I took the boys of my
class on an outing to Epping Forest: the day was overcast, but
warm and windless; the brown leaves of the previous autumn
lay in drifts underfoot and the leaves overhead were the

softest green, so soft that they seemed more an exhalation than a growth. The woods were silent, except for our own shouting and crashing through the leaves. When we came to an open space we played rounders, and then had lunch, the boys sharing with me the sandwiches that their mothers had packed for them. After lunch it grew steadily warmer; the clouds seemed to move lower, the air to become heavier. The shouts of the boys no longer carried as they had done before, among the trees, and I brought them together and made for the road and the bus-stop, anxious lest it should begin to rain. But the rain held off until we were back among the lights and traffic and cinema posters just outside the school; no sooner was the downpour over than the air was clear and bright again.

London in summer was very different to what it had been in the bleak, dark spring: in some ways a gayer, more relaxed city; in others, an even shabbier one, for the sun exposed much that was better concealed. The intensity of the difference was to me unexpected, for in South Africa—or at least in the part of South Africa from which I came—summer and winter look much alike. Here the days lengthened extravagantly, the trees continued to thicken and darken with foliage, people wore a kind of clothing they had not worn before and thronged together in the parks, whole suburbs which had previously been hidden by smoke and mist as I went on the bus to school now revealed their black and red roofs, their roads, their football fields. It seemed that in England even the calendar had visible, external meanings that I had not fully understood before. And the chief of these meanings was movement; the passage of time made manifest.

II

I had got the job at the school through Naomi K. who had known that the boys' school to which her kindergarten was attached had been looking for a class-master who could teach, among other things, English, History and French. French I could not teach, but I thought I could make an attempt to teach the rest. So, after Naomi had put in a word for me, I took a bus to Camden Town, changed there to another bus, and travelled for a further forty-five minutes through great tracts of London I had never seen before, to be interviewed by Mr B., the school secretary and its effective head.

Of Mr B. I retained an impression, from that first interview, of little more than a pair of heavy spectacles and a black beard. Later I was to see that a smile of unexpected charm could come between the beard and the spectacles. But he did not smile the first morning I saw him—not once. He was wearing a black overcoat and a hat on the back of his head; he sat at the end of a long table, piled high with papers and exercise books, pedagogic charts and old newspapers in Yiddish and English. The room was poverty-stricken; it had a bare, battered semi-public appearance, like the committee room of an unsuccessful political party or charitable appeal. The paint on the walls was pitted; the light-shade was covered in dust. A glassed-in bookcase stood in one corner, and a desk in another. That was all its furniture, apart from the laden table and a few chairs.

Mr B. laboriously wrote down in a paper-covered exercise book almost everything I said. He took down my date of birth, the school I had attended, the degree I had taken in South Africa, the fact that I had no teaching experience. He did not ask me the questions I had been afraid he might ask: What was I doing in England? How long did I think I would stay? What did I want to become? These were questions to which I had no answers; or no answers which I felt I could give to Mr B. But he did ask me whether I was orthodox; or rather, he stated as a fact, in his strong East European accent, looking through his spectacles at my bare head and clean-shaven chin, 'You are not orthodox.'

'No.'

He drew a line under the words 'Bachelor of Arts, University of the Witwatersrand, Johannesburg' and wrote: 'Not orthodox'. Then he drew a line under that. He asked me if my parents had been born in Europe. I told him that my mother was from Lithuania; that my father had spent part of his boyhood in Latvia and part in Lithuania. Which towns in Lithuania and Latvia, he asked; but he did not write down the answers.

'You speak Yiddish?'

'No. I understand it, though.'

'Hebrew?'

I told him that I'd spent about six months in Israel, and could understand a little conversational Hebrew. But that was all.

'Mrs K. tells me you can't teach French?'

'No.'

He wrote that down. Then he closed the exercise book and stared at me in silence. I didn't know what he wanted me to do or say. In the silence I became aware once again of the continual murmur overhead, that I had noticed when I had first come into the building. It was a restless, shuffling, hubbub of sound, unmistakable to anyone who had ever attended a school of any kind; as characteristic as the smell of dust, schoolbooks and chalk that was in my nostrils. Under Mr B.'s stare, hearing that noise, my heart sank. I was too close to my own schooldays to feel anything but depression at the thought of entering a school once again, in any capacity. I would have been relieved, just then, if Mr B. had told me that on considering my qualifications he had decided that I wasn't suitable for the appointment.

But he didn't say that; instead, unexpectedly, taking it for granted that the position was mine, he began explaining to me the principles on which the school was run. From eight in the morning until twelve, it was a 'Talmud Torah'. Did I know what a Talmud Torah was? The boys studied Hebrew and the Bible and the Talmud, under one group of teachers. Then, under another group, from twelve o'clock until four-thirty they studied the subjects taught in any other school. So my day would begin at twelve. I would have no duties after school hours. The salary would be six pounds ten shillings a week, and I would get a free school-lunch. He would write to me confirming the arrangement. I would begin after half-term; that is, at the beginning of the next week. He stood up, and we shook hands. Only then did he say, in a calm, warning tone, 'You will remember always that this school is here to preserve Jewish orthodoxy. You will not give offence.'

'I'll try not to.'

'Good.' He nodded, gave me a last stare through his spectacles, and turned away. I went out of the room, into the bare vestibule, then into the blighted garden in front of the school, and so on to the main road, where the buses ran.

All around the school, in every direction, there were miles of houses that must have been built at about the same time as the school itself, out of the same repulsive grey brick, with the same cream-coloured plaster along their corners and around their windows, and the same slate roofs overhead. Few of them, however, were of the size of the school, which I imagine must once have been the house of some aspiring late-Victorian or Edwardian shopkeeper or professional man. But it no longer looked the least opulent or ambitious now; it fitted in unnoticeably with the entire district, which was miserably drab, featureless, shapeless, endless, with not a building or corner you could look forward to before it came, or remember when it was past.

On the way to school there were several main crossroads, with their clusters of tiled cinemas and brick tube-stations, radio shops, fish-and-chip shops, branches of Woolworths and Marks and Spencer; there were many factories; there were a few iron subways where trains passed over the road; there were perhaps a dozen garages and motor showrooms; there were one or two little parks with green grass and soot-blackened tree-trunks; for the rest, there were just those grey brick houses, smaller or larger, dirtier or cleaner, standing on the road or held back from it by tiny gardens. Travelling up and down this route, you had a glimpse of the true size of London; at any rate it was called 'London', though you had no sense of place within it. It was a mere bulging of bricks and mortar, a distension, a continuation of what was already nothing but a continuation. And never, not even when the bus went into a lower gear and slowly climbed an incline, was there an end to it. You looked over roofs on to roofs, between streets into streets, from one sprawled suburb across the next.

The decrepitude of Paddington and Notting Hill, of the whole of central London was dramatic, or appeared to be so; it seemed to speak to one of all kinds of terrors and satisfactions, of as many of both as one's mind could imagine. But the

shabbiness of these areas on the way to school had no voice,
no accent, no meaning; at most they had a kind of pathos, which
you felt when you saw the women coming out of the pinched,
meagre, indistinguishable homes, carrying their shopping-bags
and pushing their high-wheeled prams; or when you saw into
the interiors of the little shops which the women would visit,
with the tins of groceries piled on shelves, and men in aprons
leaning over counters, their hands clasped idly together and
their gaze quite still but seeing nothing.

And here, in the middle of all this, barely a hundred yards
away from one of the busiest of the road-junctions, was the
—— School, devoted to the preservation of Jewish orthodoxy.
Every weekday morning the boys assembled, looking much like
English schoolboys from any poor district, with their caps on
their heads, their scarves around their necks and their bare
knees showing through their open raincoats; they said their
prayers and settled down to study the Bible and the Talmud.
They watched television whenever they could; they read comics
and exchanged them with one another; they debated about the
merits of motor cars and jet planes; they went to the cinema as
often as they were permitted; they followed the fortunes of their
favourite football teams. But they never went to watch football,
because most of the games were played on the Sabbath; many
of them didn't cut the hair over their temples because that was
forbidden by the Law they studied; they didn't buy ice-cream
from the carts in the streets because it wasn't kosher; they
never took their caps off in class, let alone in the street; they
wore *tzitzith* under their vests; they prayed at all odd hours of
the day, with antique gestures; they believed literally in every
word of the Bible—or tried to believe in every word of it.
They were heroic, absurd, and maddening.

I was not a great success as a teacher. I don't think I would
have been, anyway, with any boys, because of my youth, my
lack of conviction in myself in the role, and my uncertainty
about some of the subjects I was supposed to be teaching.
And because of my South African accent, which the boys—who
themselves spoke with the oddest mixture of Cockney and
Yiddish accents—all found unceasingly amusing, and which I

used to hear them imitating whenever I was out of the class-room. ('Na,' I'd hear them saying, 'we'll furst do histry; awfter histry, meths.') But what told most against me was simply that I was, in their eyes, an apostate. Many of them refused to believe at first that I was Jewish; when, in response to their questioning, I insisted that I was, they bombarded me with other questions. Why didn't I wear a hat, or at least a *kappel*? Did I shave every day? Did I eat pork? *Why* did I call myself a Jew? Did I go to *shul*? Didn't I believe in God? Wasn't I frightened of what would happen to me, if I went on breaking the Law?

I answered those questions I thought I could answer ('without offence'); I ignored the rest. But they were satisfied neither by my answers nor by my silences. And I was always betraying my ignorance and apostasy in other ways. I interrupted boys at prayer, not knowing that they were at prayer. I told them to kneel when we were doing a class play-reading of *Henry IV Part I*, which was their set Shakespeare. ('Sir!' they cried out in horror, 'only *goyim* kneel!') I absent-mindedly told a boy to take his cap off when he spoke to me. I revealed that I'd been to the theatre on a Friday evening, that I rode on a bus on a Saturday. I wasn't sure of the sequence in which the holy-days came round, and knew the significance of only the more important ones. I had never studied Talmud; the only Hebrew I knew was corrupt and slangy (these boys believed it to be sinful to use Hebrew for any but religious purposes); I didn't know the details of the laws of *kashrut*. The boys used to enjoy enlightening and correcting me, they used to enjoy even their own sense of outrage at my lapsed, ignorant state; but their corrections and cries of outrage weren't a help in maintaining discipline.

And yet, somehow, we managed—managed almost as well as anyone else did in the school, I suspect. Its organisation was chaotic; so much so that one could hardly talk of it having any organisation at all. I was never given a syllabus, a time-table, a register; there was a chronic shortage of books and pencils and chalk to write with on the single, scarred black-board. At irregular intervals—sometimes twice a week, sometimes once a week, and in some weeks not at all—Mr B.

would come in to give my boys French; the rest of the time I was left to do what I liked with them. We went through the arithmetic books and the geometry primer that they swore they had been through twice already, with other teachers; we worked our way through the English grammar books that some of them seemed to know off by heart. And what books they were —physically, I mean—ancient, coverless, dogeared scraps of things, literally bewhiskered where the stitching along their spines had unravelled, illustrated on every page by schoolboy drawings, held together by glue and scotch tape. They were collected by the 'books monitor' (a position eagerly competed for) at the end of each lesson, and piled in the cupboard, along with the Hebrew books, in rather better condition, which were also stored there, and the unclaimed caps and broken schoolbags thrust into a corner.

There were no geography books, no history books, no science books, no nature study books; but I was expected to teach them history and geography, nature study and science, all the same. I was also expected to teach them drawing, though I had no talent at all for drawing. Inevitably, under these circumstances, we spent much of our time simply talking to one another; or I read them stories. *Treasure Island* was a huge success; it used almost to frighten me, when I would look up and see in their rapt, fixed, hungry eyes, even in the strained tendons of their necks, the effect the book was having on them. *Gulliver's Travels* was much less of a success, I remember, and *Tom Sawyer*, too, was rather a disappointment; they enjoyed many of the details, but the story as a whole didn't hold their attention.

But even in the formal lessons, there were times when I felt that we exchanged something of value with one another; and there were a few boys with whom I felt this often. One I remember with especial fondness was a tall, bespectacled boy with long plump limbs and a mild, indifferent manner, who wrote the best essays in the class, and spelt the most atrociously. I suspected him of being a secret liberal, among all the other young fanatics. But almost any of the boys at one time or another would reveal an unexpected interest, or manage to come out with a genuinely witty remark (they all came out continuously, compulsively, with would-be witty remarks), or would just give a sigh of pleasure at his own insight when some point I was trying to make would suddenly become clear to him, or a sum he was doing would come out, or one fact would remind him of another he hadn't previously connected with it.

And there were a few, of course, with whom it was impossible to make any contact at all. It was humiliating to find that their malice was equal, invariably, to their capacity to enrage. I would tell myself that I would not be provoked by them— next time; that I would treat coolly and effectively their impertinence or insolence, or their studied, idle sabotage of the lessons. But at some crucial moment in a lesson, just when I felt I had at last succeeded in rousing the curiosity of the class, one of the malicious ones would let fly with a paper dart, or would start scratching noisily at his desk with a razor blade, or would hold his nose ostentatiously and fan his hand in the air, to indicate to everyone around him that someone had farted. And I would forget my resolutions and hear my voice rise in rage; hot, embarrassed, and without dignity, I would see the class escape from me in the resulting excitement— whether or not I succeeded in imposing silence on them—and the lesson would be in ruins.

One of the worst offenders was a small, swarthy boy with the longest and most pious *payess* in the class; he used to wear them curled back behind his ears, like the earpieces of a pair of spectacles. Considering his appearance, that boy was altogether a surprise. When the summer came I used to take my class to play cricket, one afternoon a week, in a near-by park, and he proved himself to be a brilliant natural batsman, with a superb sense of timing and a classic way of using his feet. He used to knock my bowling all over the field, much to the pleasure of the others. And there was another boy who was an especial torment to me: a twitcher, a liar, a retailer of dirty jokes, a puller of faces. Secretly, I suspected him of being a little mad; I was sure there were times when he gibbered and pulled his faces not in order to annoy me, but simply because he couldn't help himself. I once suggested to Mr B. that he should be sent to a child guidance clinic; but the suggestion was received so coldly I didn't make it again. Eventually he was caught chalking the wall along the street with the words 'This is a rotten school' in letters twelve inches high; and from then on it was agreed that he was, in fact, a problem-case. But so far as I knew nothing was ever done about him.

The boys were all poor: the poverty of the school was chronic, irremediable. The signs of poverty I had seen in Mr B.'s office on my first visit were repeated in the staff-room, which was as long, bare and as cluttered with papers as the office; in every classroom; in the lavatories and lobbies; in the small asphalted playground at the back. There wasn't a carpet or a bit of linoleum in the place; not a plastered wall that wasn't cracked and defaced with scribblings, not a clean window, not a desk that wasn't battered, a bookcase that wasn't split along its sides and half-filled with books in the same condition as those in my class; there wasn't a floorboard that didn't yield with a sigh or groan when you stepped on it, or the tread of a stair that wasn't worn away into a kind of splintered concavity; there wasn't a door that hung straight in its frame or a door-handle that didn't turn uselessly in your grasp; not a blade of grass in the front-garden, not a single piece of equipment in the playground at the back. Even the bat we played cricket with was dry and splintered, like one of those stairs, and the buckles of the pads had long been lost and replaced with bits of string. Black, tubular iron stoves which scorched when you stood near them and gave no warmth when you stepped away from them were the sole source of heating in the school; dusty, unshaded light-bulbs hanging from encrusted pieces of flex provided the only light when the day was overcast. Everything was grey, black, brown, dirty cream—the colours of penury.

Every Friday, soon after lunch, Mr B. used to come into my class and call for two or three boys, who owned bicycles and whose parents were regular in their payment of fees, to go out to collect money from parents who had fallen behind. This was done so that the masters could be paid at the end of the afternoon. We always closed a half-hour earlier on Friday afternoons, to give the boys time to get home and wash and change before the Sabbath.

I saw very little of the members of the staff on the religious side of the school; they were always leaving the building as I came in, and I never had much occasion to do anything but nod at them as they passed in a succession of black hats, black beards and pale faces. I saw very little, too, of the titular head of the school, who was a portly, venerable figure, dressed in the inevitable black hat and black overcoat, but distinguished from the others both by his size and by the whiteness of his beard. He seldom came to the school and could apparently speak very little English. When he did come he depended on Mr B. for all the information that came to him; he asked questions and nodded deeply, with his eyes closed, at the replies Mr B. gave to him; he came into the classrooms and tweaked the ear of this or that boy, asked the boy's name, and said, 'Good, good'; from the window of my classroom, I would see him make his way out of the school, umbrella clutched firmly, half-way down its length, in his hand.

Mr B. was not only the school secretary; he also taught in the mornings and, often, in the afternoons as well; it was he who took my class for French, when he could. Apart from him, the staff teaching the secular subjects consisted of one rabbinical student, from Jews' College, two would-be business men, and myself. The would-be business men were both orthodox, but only one of them was successful—the bigger, noisier, better-dressed one. He was in 'the import-export'; that is, an uncle of his who lived in Vienna, and had apparently manufactured the stuff before the war, sent him samples of artificial jewellery, make-up sets, cigarette cases, novelties and trinkets of all kinds, and he went round jewellers' stores, trying to book orders. He had no capital and could carry no stocks, so the building up of his business was a slow job for him; but his uncle's name was a good one in Vienna, he said, and there were firms who were beginning now to let them have credit. He confidently expected to leave off teaching soon, and go into business full-time.

He carried on his business as some demonstrative men carry on their love-affairs. He was always talking about it, showing us his lines, boasting to us about the orders he had managed to book, describing his customers. It would have been unpleasant, had he not been so enthusiastic and naive about it; had he not got so much obvious pleasure from it all. He had pet names for his business, he had little songs about it. I know that must sound unlikely, but it is true. 'Novelties,' he would sing, 'are the life for me/Novelties are the life for you/We will make a fortune from little novelties.' He sang jingles like this in the staff-room, slapping his hands together and sucking his breath between his teeth. He referred to his business when he spoke to us as 'Noveltibirds' or 'Knick-Knack-Novelties' or 'Mickey Marcasite'; but its name on his stationery was exaltedly English in character: something like Marlborough Importers Limited. One lunch-hour, as a great treat, he took me to his office, which was above a row of dingy shops, at the end of a ten-minute bus-ride away from the school. There he pointed out to me his filing-cabinet, and his desk; he showed me the samples he kept locked in a cupboard; he ran his fingers like a pianist over his little portable typewriter. 'Nice?' he asked me, as proud as a child. He was by far the happiest man, or boy, at —— School.

Poor Y. wasn't such a success as a business man. It was because of the apparent success of the other that he too had tried to go into 'the import-export'. He had written to various manufacturers of socks and ties and girls' drawers in Italy, and had asked to be appointed their London agent. One or two had responded, and had sent him samples; on the strength of these he was trying to book orders from clothing and haber-dashery stores. But he wasn't doing well. At the end of term, wretchedly embarrassed, he approached me and asked if I would like to buy some of his samples. He showed me what he had of them in his briefcase. I agreed to buy a couple of pairs of green socks. The transaction took place in the staff-room; I can still see Y.'s small, pale face, with a bush of curly brown hair growing boyishly above it, as he implored me not to tell any of the others about my purchase. He pocketed the money I gave him, and stuffed the socks into a brown paper-bag before handing them over to me.

It wasn't really surprising that Y. disliked S., the successful one, so much; and used to accuse him of shirking his duties, spying for the school secretary, and thinking of nothing but money. But he never made these accusations in S.'s presence; instead, they used to have interminable, futile arguments about things they had seen on the television or read in the newspapers. If S. had enjoyed a programme, Y. said he'd hated it; if S. thought the accused in a current murder-trial innocent, then Y. said he was guilty; if S. prophesied a war anywhere on the globe, Y. insisted nothing would happen.

The rabbinical student and I were frequently called upon to adjudicate in these disputes; both of us did our best to remain aloof from them. The rabbinical student was invariably quiet in the staff-room. He wore rimless fragile glasses, and a fluff of gingery beard on his chin; he smiled often, at nothing in particular. I don't think he and I exchanged more than twenty sentences, that weren't connected with work, in the months I was at the school. Looking back now, it seems rather strange that none of them showed any particular curiosity about me; they didn't ask me what I was doing in England, or whether I intended making a career out of teaching. Nor did they ever ask me to their homes. At the time I put down their lack of curiosity to the fact that they were all refugees, who had come to England just before or during the war; compared to their own, my reasons for having come to England (whatever they assumed them to be) must have seemed frivolous.

III

In England, it became clear to me that, through England, I wanted to escape from the ironies, ambiguities and humiliations of my own position as a Jew, as a white South African, as a 'colonial', as a young man who didn't know what to do with his life. I wanted in some way to share in the country's strength; to take into myself something of the power I saw deployed in its books and buildings, its institutions and industries, in the complexity of its arrangements and the simplicity of the ideas it most liked to hold about itself.

In return, I was prepared to give what I could. As I wandered around London I felt a protective concern for the country, which was at the same time a kind of awe, even a kind of reverence, towards it. This emotion was associated particularly in my mind with the thought of the last war; and I remember feeling it most strongly outside St Paul's one morning, looking over the devastation around the cathedral. Only a few blocks of buildings rose irregularly to any height; over most of the area there were just footpaths across the bomb-sites, running between low walls like hedges. One really felt oneself to be standing on a hilltop, looking down over the ruins of a city, as an archaeologist might be able to see it. And I found myself thinking over and over, 'Don't let this happen again. Don't let this happen again.' I was not directing this injunction to anyone in particular, as far as I knew; it was simply a kind of amateur prayer, addressed to history in general.

But I would not have cared nearly so much, I knew, if I hadn't thought England rich, grand, and imposing as well as vulnerable; if, to give the most obvious example of the grandness I mean, the great black bubble of the dome of St Paul's had not swelled itself in the air directly behind me, over the injured landscape. Weakness and destitution would not have been able to rouse my protective instinct in this way; if I hadn't been filled with admiration and wonder, I would not have been filled with solicitude either.

Wonder: anything in those days could be an occasion for wonder. I just had to look at the windows of the buildings in London—the windows merely—to be overwhelmed by a sense of the richness and diversity of the life that had achieved its embodiment in England. In South Africa a window was oblong, square or round, framed in steel or wood. And that was all, that exhausted the varieties of windows and the interest you could get from them. But on my very first morning in London I had noticed the vertical, fan-like setting of brick above each window in the Bloomsbury terraces, so that they all looked rather like eyes, with eyebrows raised in faint surprise; later that same morning, when I went to my bank near South Africa House, I saw that the windows of the Victorian office blocks along Northumberland Avenue were surrounded by pilasters, by terra cotta fruits, by ribbons and wreaths. From then on it became almost a nervous habit of mine to glance at the windows of buildings; and every kind of window I saw seemed to have its own distinctive character, its own kind of arch, bay, surround, recess, sill, lintel, pediment, and a hundred other features for which I had no words, at which I could merely stare before moving on.

And this was to look, briefly enough, at few enough windows! The country seemed to me so full, so packed with life, that again and again I couldn't help feeling that if I were just to close my hand in the air, I would grasp more than air: I would find between my fingers a texture, a colour, a weight.

Once I had settled into my job at the school I used to go much less often to the West End; usually I went in only on Friday evenings, after I'd been paid for my work. When I had been delayed at school I would arrive at Piccadilly Circus or Leicester Square just as the rush-hour began; and it used to be part of my Friday evening's entertainment simply to stand at the foot of the packed escalators of these stations, looking up at the crowds descending. Always it seemed as though they were about to topple and fall down the steep incline, of their own sheer weight; one felt dizzy standing beneath them, watching the endless human chain wheel over and come down towards one. And no matter how quickly the people stepped from the stairs and hurried away once they had reached the bottom, the wedge on the escalator remained solid, unbroken, it filled entirely the space that was given to it.

Altogether, the London underground was one of the great sights of the city for me. I had never imagined that it would be so complex; that I would spend as much of my time in it as I did; that it would dispose of such huge numbers of people; that it would have its characteristic architecture, light, air, smells, noises, and impose upon the people who travelled in it a characteristic expression of the face; that the stations would be so much alike and yet differ so much from one another, and from themselves at different times of the day. In fact, while I was still unfamiliar with it—before it became merely common-place, an indifferent and uncomfortable passage through which I had to make my way so many times a week—the underground seemed to me a symbol or image of a kind that was all the more portentous for being so obscure. It was impossible for me to keep out of my mind all sorts of half-ideas about purgatory and the after-life, as I bewilderedly made my way through one subterranean tunnel to the next, among the hurrying crowds, bent upon their own destinations; yet, at the same time, the underground appeared to be the true centre or source of the city's life, rather than an image of its death. One felt inside it, more so than anywhere else, as though London were nothing but a great machine, contracting and expanding to its own deep, mechanical rhythms; a machine which the people who lived in London did not control but merely had to obey. So they were brought together and hurled apart again, as the machine dictated. But even to think of the machine 'dictating' to the anonymous crowds made it seem too personal. The machine itself did not know what it was doing: it merely flashed its lights, moved its stairs, sent its trains hurtling along grey, ribbed tunnels, festooned with cables; its servants cried out 'Mind the gap' above the sigh of closing doors and the shuffling sound of the passengers' feet, above the thunderous fading roar of other trains in other tunnels. Sometimes the machine breathed in gales that cut through one's clothing, at other times the air hung still and oppressively warm; sometimes the trains stopped in mid-tunnel and waited in a humming silence before moving on again; at times the platforms and the moving stairs were deserted, and yet the trains still emerged and departed, the stairs rattled and folded in and out of each other. And all this vast activity and movement seemed to serve no purpose but that of its own continuation, could not serve any other purpose, for there was no consciousness that guided or directed it.

I used to wonder, at first, why there were so few literary references to the underground; before I learned to take it for granted, I wondered why everyone else did. In fact, there was one writer I knew of who had used it in his work, and it is partly for this reason, and not only because of what he has written about the City, that T. S. Eliot has remained for me pre-eminently the poet of London; as much London's poet as Dickens is still its novelist.

Anyway, on these Friday evenings I would emerge from the underground station and make straight for the theatre of my choice. There I would book a stool in the gallery queue, and then I would try to fill in the time that remained until the theatre opened. Usually, I just walked around the West End and Soho, and looked at shop-windows and people, or grubbed among the second-hand books in the Charing Cross Road; I went a few times to the National Gallery; I ate some kind of a meal in a Lyons tea-room. I was always early for the theatre, and was often enough glad to get into it simply to rest my feet.

The cocooned, cosy plush and gilt of the theatres, their ornate chandeliers and braided, pink lightshades in clusters here and there on the walls, were all novelties and yet familiar from the descriptions I had read of them; they were 'sights' in much the same way as the faces of the actors and actresses I had seen previously only on the cinema screen. As much as when I walked in the streets, I was sightseeing at the theatre. But this was not the only reason why I went so regularly. I hoped earnestly, devoutly, to discover in myself a passion for the theatre of the kind I had so often read about. I wanted to feel in myself that 'hush of expectancy' when the 'house-lights were dimmed'; to 'store up for myself' memories of 'enchanted evenings' and 'unforgettable performances'; to be one of those 'young people' whose 'devotion to the theatre' helped to 'keep it alive'—not with the money they spent on their seats in 'the gods' but with their 'discriminating taste' and 'undimmed enthusiasm'.

It goes almost without saying that I cannot now remember a single one of the plays I saw; not a title, not a plot, not a joke, not a stage-setting. All I can remember are my own efforts to persuade myself into an enthusiasm I was never really able to convince myself I felt. That I should have put so much effort into a hopeless endeavour—and one which I now feel it would have been shameful to have succeeded in—shows, I suppose, just how little I knew about myself, or the London theatre.

Of course, I hoped also that up there in 'the gods' I would meet some beautiful, young, sincere, lonely, ardent, female theatre-lover, and that a friendship, and more than a friend-ship, would develop between us. Actually, the closest I came to it was to see several times at various theatres a quite pretty

girl, who came to recognize me, and who I think would have
welcomed an approach from me. What held me back was that
this girl was always accompanied by her quite youthful and
quite goodlooking mother—which was something my fantasies
had never bargained for. I couldn't possibly tackle them both,
of that I was sure; so the girl and I never did more than
exchange a few uncertain smiles.

In the novels I read, young men in the position I was in
were continually picking up attractive girls in streets and
parks and bookshops; I had no such luck. As a matter of fact,
of the people I have since known in London, only one has
seemed able to do it again and again. This man found his girls
for the most part in coffee-bars, which weren't in existence my
first year in London, and in museums, which I hardly ever
visited. But I doubt if I'd have been very much more successful
even if coffee-bars had been in existence and had I made a
habit of frequenting museums. I hadn't the knack. All I did
have was a host of images of the girl I would eventually meet:
sometimes she was English, sometimes South African; sometimes she was Jewish, sometimes Gentile; sometimes she was
tall, sometimes slight; sometimes she was dark, sometimes fair;
sometimes she was sophisticated, sometimes naïve; invariably,
she was generous, high-spirited, and compliant. But because I
was without friends, visited no homes, went to no parties, it
seemed that I had no chance of meeting her—though all too
often I would catch a glimpse of her, in a crowd of other girls,
or on the arm of another man.

And always, everywhere, I felt myself to be touched, nudged,
pulled by the sexual underworld of London; an underworld
much wider than that of the whores who stood on every West
End corner after nightfall, or of the homosexuals hanging about
outside the mens' lavatories in Leicester Square and Trafalgar
Square tube-stations. These the newspapers wrote about every
weekend; but they never said a word about the furtive en-
counters and withdrawals that took place in darkened, half-
empty cinemas; about the rubber-shops with their dangling
trusses, books on flagellation, and their offers to send you
'further literature' in 'plain wrappers'; about the wild, imploring
graffiti scribbled upon the doors and walls of practically every

B*

public lavatory; about the packed tube-trains, where the crowds swayed promiscuously against one another, heads respectably averted, bodies rammed together. Or, for that matter, about the sedate, secluded middle-class house in which I lodged, and in which almost every room seemed filled with whispers that sometimes rose to cries, sniggers, sobs, expostulations, behind the closed doors.

I knew none of the people who lodged in the house; we passed each other on the stairs, and greeted one another, and that was all. And yet it surprises me now to realize just how much I did learn about them; at least about those who lived on my landing. There was, for example, the Danish student (so-called: he was much older in looks than any student had the right to be) in the room next door to mine. His girl spent one week in his room crying almost continuously, and then left for Australia: that I guessed from the silence which descended upon his room when the week was over, and from the Australian air-letters addressed to him, in a feminine hand, which shortly afterwards began to appear on the window-ledge where the housekeeper left all our letters. Had she threatened to go to Australia unless he married her? Or was she Australian, and had she wept simply because she had to go home and he wouldn't follow her? In any case, the Scandinavian did not pine for her. The last girl had cried; his new one laughed. I would hear the deep, gurgling sound of her laughter at all hours of the night—above the sound of Radio Luxembourg, to which their radio seemed to be permanently tuned.

The room next to mine on the other side was occupied by an elderly German Jewish widow, whose daughter, I gathered from overheard snatches of conversation in German and English, was unhappily married. The daughter complained to her mother about her husband's stinginess with money, his angry moods, his absences; the mother counselled patience. I saw the husband a few times on the stairs: a tall, fair, high-coloured man, with the face of a disgruntled boy. To judge from his accent, he too was a German Jew, but he always spoke in English. He had almost as many complaints against his wife as she had against him; and what was very odd about his way of delivering these complaints was that he seemed to take it for granted that his mother-in-law would agree with him. 'She's impossible, isn't she?' he would say in conclusion to his mother-in-law about her daughter, or, 'What can you do with someone like that, tell me, please.' These confrontations took place about once a week (the daughter came three or four times a week), and usually ended up with the three of them going, at the mother's suggestion, to the pictures.

Across the landing there lived the quietest of the couples on my floor: a tall well-spoken Englishman in his middle thirties, who went off every morning in a dark suit and bowler hat to the bank or insurance office in which he worked, and his small, curly-headed Cypriot boy-friend. The Cypriot was apparently supported by his friend and seldom went out; he used to potter about the house, and have long conversations with the housekeeper, and listen to the soap-operas on the radio. When he did go out he wore clothes of a very different kind from those of his friend: striped shirts, black jeans, belts with big silver buckles. The two of them seemed staid and settled, and I shall never know why the Englishman suddenly left; certainly, there had been no loud rows before his departure.

It must have been just two or three days after the Englishman had left that the Cypriot knocked on my door. He had come with a suggestion, or an invitation. Wouldn't I move in with him? We had never done more than greet one another, as I have said, or exchange a few remarks about the weather. Now he stood with his back against the wall, a pace away from the door, and smiled at me guilelessly. 'It's a fine room,' he said. 'It's too dear for me. But with you—with the two of us—it's easy.' And he made a gesture with his hand, twisting the palm of it open, towards me. The gesture seemed somehow both obscene and touching. Still he smiled; he was a round-cheeked, brown-eyed boy, with white teeth and dark curls that fell all over his forehead. I wondered with some alarm what it was about me that had made him think I might be a successor to that departed Englishman. 'No, thank you,' I said. 'It's kind of you to ask me, but——'

'See the room?' he suggested. 'It's much bigger than this one. We can be comfortable there, you wait and see. I do all the work in the room. I keep it clean, I can cook, I look after everything.' Hastily, I said that I was preparing for an examination, I studied in the evenings, and couldn't possibly consider sharing with anyone.

'Oh,' he assured me, his smile even more artless than before, 'I can be very quiet.'

I simply shook my head in silence, looking at him; my gaze, I'm sure, was far more embarrassed than the one he met it with. But he was very polite; almost condescending. He shrugged, said he hoped I didn't mind that he'd asked me, and slid out of the room. A few days later he was gone. His room was then occupied by a couple of girl-students, one of whom I thought very attractive in the soft, eager, earnest, innocent way that characterises so many English girl-students. Even when you know nothing about them or their circumstances, girls like these somehow make you feel that you should sympathize with their views and admire their pluck. I looked forward to meeting this girl on the stairs; when we did meet I tried to make our conversation last as long as possible. But the development of our friendship was cut short by an unfortunate accident. All the people on my landing shared a single, huge bathroom-cum-lavatory. One afternoon I opened the door of this room; and there, on the lavatory seat, sat the girl, with her pants around her ankles. She had forgotten to lock the door behind her. For the briefest and most protracted of seconds we stared at one another; then she gave a kind of moan, and reached down towards her ankles, while I retreated, muttering apologies and banging the door closed behind me.

From then on the poor girl couldn't say a word to me. When she saw me she blushed, she ducked, she scurried away down the passage or up the stairs. As long as I lived in the house she never forgave me, or herself, for what had happened.

When I had told the Cypriot that I was working for an examination I had been telling a lie. But it was true that I was working almost every evening, at this time. I had begun writing, in earnest—or so I thought. At any rate, what drove me to start working seemed earnest enough to me.

I was still seeing the K.'s and G. and his girl-friend, on

alternate weeks; in addition there was a girl whom I had known at university in Johannesburg whom I saw even more infrequently; there were friends of K. and G. with whom I spent occasional evenings. Generally, what this meant was that in every week I was in the company of others one evening and one weekend afternoon; the other six nights, the rest of the weekends, I was on my own. And I was no longer able to fill them, as I'd been able to at first, simply by being on the move. Loneliness had had its pleasures; there had been something extraordinarily satisfying, at times, in the thought that none of the people who ever saw me knew who I was; conversely, there was a kind of exhilaration in the thought that at any given moment none of the people who *did* know me could guess just where I was, what I was doing, where I would go next. But I found that these moments of excitement or self-satisfaction were recurring less and less frequently. And I had begun to have fears that were worse than those mild hallucinations or displacements that I'd been afflicted with in my first few weeks in the city, when again and again, in broad daylight, I had found myself thinking I was back in Johannesburg, or had made a habit of 'recognizing' people who in fact were complete strangers to me. Chiefly, I was afraid now of falling ill or having an accident. 'It could be weeks before anyone would even know!'— that seemed to be the real horror of the situation.

Actually, I was exaggerating the forlornness of my own position. Now that I was working, any absence of mine would certainly have been noticed; and, after a very few days Mr B. would have gone over to the nursery-department of the school (which was run, by the way, quite independently from his) and would have asked Naomi what had happened to me. And Naomi would, I'm sure, have taken the trouble to come to my room to find out. But what could she have done for me if she did come? And what if I wasn't there? What if I was in some hospital, miles away—unconscious, perhaps? It didn't occur to me that in that case I would then be unconscious of my own loneliness as well; but I doubt if the thought would have been of much comfort anyway. Nor did I find it much of a comfort to remind myself that my health had so far been excellent, and showed no signs of deteriorating suddenly.

Still, it's always easy to be superior to one's own anxieties when one no longer feels them; and the truth is that if I had fallen ill I would probably have had a thoroughly miserable time of it. In the best of health, I was finding my loneliness quite heavy enough a burden, anyway. It was at this time, I remember, that the notices which used to be posted up outside Tottenham Court Road police-station began to have a macabre fascination for me. 'Found: in Thames, near Greenwich, body of man, aged 20-23, wearing brown sports jacket and grey flannels, height 5' 7", scar on right cheek. . . .' 'Found: 63 —— Crescent N.W., body of woman, aged 50 years approx. . . .' To prevent such a notice ever being posted up about me, I wrote my name and parents' address in South Africa on a piece of paper, and put it in my wallet. It embarrassed me to do this, I remember; but I did it, nevertheless.

So I stayed in my room more than ever before; it seemed to me I was safer there than anywhere else. And because I had to do something while I was in my room, I began to write a novel. However, if I began work on it as a means of self-defence, it wasn't long before I thought of the book as my attack: as the instrument with which I would subdue the city beyond the walls of my room. I had no precise idea of what London would look like to me once it was subdued; but I was sure, at least, that it would seem a very different place from what it did then. Months later I finished the novel, and was glad to put it quietly out of sight. London had changed for me, in the meantime; but not as a result of anything that novel had ever done to it, or ever would.

One afternoon I came home early from school—I forget why—and found a little girl waiting on the doorstep. She had come for her dancing-lesson (the ground-floor of the house was still occupied by the school of dancing); she told me, while I looked through my pockets for my key, that her daddy had brought her in his car, and that he was going to fetch her when the lesson was over. She said she'd been ringing at the door-bell but no one had answered it.

At the time I wasn't struck by the oddity of this; usually, on afternoons when the lessons were held in the house, the front-door was simply left wide open. I cannot remember what the little girl looked like, except that she had freckles on her face, and that like all the little girls who came for their classes she carried her dancing-shoes in a small cloth bag. What I do recall was that her voice was sweet and clear, and that I was touched by the volubility with which she chattered to me during the minute or two we stood together on the step. As it happened, I really had to hunt for my key, in every pocket, before I finally found it. Then I opened the door, and I know that I felt rather pleased with myself for having been able to help her. Once we were inside I simply went straight up the stairs, and she very politely called after me, from the big, gloomy lobby of the house, 'Good-bye. Thank you.' I replied to her without looking back.

How long it was before she called to me again, I cannot now say. Indeed, in many ways the whole incident has the quality of a bad dream for me; except that I know, to my regret, that it wasn't a dream, that it actually happened. I think that I settled down to read, once I was in my room, or perhaps I just lay on my bed; in any case, I remained awake. It seems almost unbelievable to me now that I could have sat or lain there, in that dead-silent house, without thinking that something was amiss. But I know quite well how I did it. I had simply forgotten about the little girl; I'd smiled at her, and listened to her chatter, and opened the door for her, and then she had just gone out of my mind, as though I'd never seen her. So much so that I didn't even think of her when I heard a child's voice calling out, of all things, 'I'm only seven.'

I thought the call came from somewhere outside in the street; it struck me as rather a strange thing for a child to shout out, but I assumed it was some part of a game or an argument. Afterwards, that first call struck me as being as pitiful as anything that followed; it showed so clearly how the girl's own puniness, in that enormous, silent house, must have been borne in upon her. But I wasn't thinking of her, then. That first call was followed by a long silence; and then by a truly terrifying shriek: 'Mister man! Help me! I don't know my way home! You're my friend!' A moment later the front door shut with a bang that shook the entire house.

And only then, when it was too late, I realized that it was

the little girl that I'd let into the house who had called; that it was to *me* that she was calling. Immediately, I knew what had happened; I should have known before I had opened the door which shouldn't have been closed; I should certainly have known when I had left the child in that still, empty lobby. There was no dancing-lesson that afternoon; it had been cancelled for some reason, and her parents had either not been told or had forgotten, and had dropped her at the gate as usual. And then I had let her in. And there was not a soul in the house apart from myself; by some mischance everyone was out—the housekeeper, the widow, the girl-students, everyone. The little girl had sat alone there in the half-darkness, and waited, and waited, until she had been overwhelmed by the terror of her situation. But she hadn't forgotten me in the way that I'd forgotten her; she had cried out to me, once, and again in a shriek, calling me her friend, and then, before I could do anything, driven by her own fears, had simply fled from the house.

Her friend! And I was the one who had brought her into the house, and had ignored her first cry for help! I was down the stairs in an instant, and out in the street. I looked up the slope of the hill; there was no one to be seen that way. The distance the other way, down to the Finchley Road, was only about fifty yards; I was sure she must have made for it, though I could not see her, and I ran down to the corner. It was hopeless. The pavements of Finchley Road were crowded with people, throngs of them, advancing and retreating, pausing, hurrying forward, turning aside; in the road itself trucks ground their gears, moved forward, stood idle, their exhaust fumes rising in the air. There wasn't a sign of the little girl. I ran half a block in one direction, turned and ran back in the other. She was gone, lost in the crowd. In the months that followed I looked for her many times, when the children gathered in groups outside the house before or after their lessons, but she was never among them.

IV

I'm afraid I have no conclusion to these recollections. I lived as I have tried to describe for about four months; then, as a result of a visit to some South African friends who had settled in Yorkshire, and a visit, during the summer holidays, to others who had come to live in Cambridge, the circumstances of my life in London changed greatly—changed permanently, I might say. The period I've written about had no definable consequences: simply, it was what it was, while it lasted, and then it was over.

If it left me with anything at all, it left me with questions rather than conclusions. I had hoped that somehow my life would be made more simple for me, in England; but precisely because I was so much attracted to the country, I saw quite clearly that in fact it had complicated things all the more. Now, whatever I was to do with myself, wherever I went, I knew that there would be one more term I would have to add to my guesses or calculations. One way or another, I wouldn't be able to shake England altogether from me; of that I was sure. But what I would do about this England with which I seemed now to be stuck, how I might live in it or why I might decide not to do so—these questions were merely presented to me, not answered.

And there were other questions about England—less personal, possibly, but puzzling and bewildering enough—that I was forced to ask myself. Overall, what had impressed me most about the English scene was its sheer *density*; by contrast, the South African scene, when I looked back on it, seemed not only new and bare, but haphazard, unformulated, uncertain, unrealized —its parts lacked style, lacked accommodation, lacked depth. Aware of this contrast between the two countries, seeing and feeling it wherever I went in England, the question I had to ask myself about it was this: What difference does it make? Or rather, to be more precise: What moral difference does it make? Possessing this density, or being possessed by it, were the English, quite simply, better people? Were they cleverer, did they make greater use of their own human potentialities, were they happier, were they deeper in feeling, more compassionate, more hopeful?

One answer was obvious. Clearly, people were people wherever they were; intelligence and stupidity, good and evil, did not have geographical locations. After all, I could travel just a very few miles eastwards and find myself in countries as ancient, as dense socially, as England, where just a very few years previously I would have ended my life jammed into a chamber with hundreds like myself, gasping for air and breathing in Zyklon-B. We could fill more and more elaborately and densely the space we occupied, we could accumulate buildings and develop the most subtle and refined modes of expression; but we couldn't accumulate wisdom, we couldn't lift ourselves up from what we were. All that England, all that Europe, offered to someone like myself were certain aesthetic satisfactions which I could not have found at home. Though they gratified the eye and ear, the richness, fullness and variety of England, which had come to me as such a revelation, did nothing and could do nothing to improve the minds or morals of individual Englishmen.

An obvious answer, I have said; but if I tried to realize its implications I was left feeling heartsick and cheated; I was left with the conviction that history was a malicious fraud, and that so was art. They both pretended to be so much more than mere spectacles, they hinted at meanings, purposes, resolutions; but the one stumbled and staggered from event to event, from disaster to disaster, recording everything and remembering nothing, always striving to accomplish the same ends and always astonished by its miserable failure to do so; the other had not yet succeeded in lifting from us one item of the burden of confusion and ignorance we carried. Then what was the good of them? Or of having their accumulations around us? What help did they give us? Was the choice between an old country and a new one nothing but the choice between different kinds of amusement or diversion? And was one diverted always from the same horror of inertia, recurrence, and aimlessness beneath?

Yet, on another level, a different answer was as obvious as the first one I had given. England *was* a happier country than South Africa, a more gentle and hopeful country. And it seemed to me a great achievement that England should have managed to combine with its power so much benignity. Somehow, through a series of accidents and chances (and through the efforts, surely, of numberless individual Englishmen) something, it seemed, had been learned in England; something had been lifted, however insecurely and temporarily, above the wash and ebb of recurrence. What that 'something' was I couldn't define, though I had many different words for it: endurance, concern, readiness, patience, restraint, earnestness. Whatever it was, the English found it difficult to take with them when they went overseas; at home, another war or a time of hunger would overthrow it; even in times of peace and comparative plenty it was clear that the English themselves frequently resented having to live with it, and expressed their resentment in a meanness, a rancour, or an offhand rudeness that were characteristically their own. And yet, it remained: a moral temper without which England would have been a different country— and the world I had my chance of living in a bleaker place.

1961/1962

AFTER NOTTING HILL

THE WALLS OF THE court were white, the chairs on which the judge and counsel sat were heavy affairs of green leather, with a gold crest emblazoned on each. The judge himself was be-wigged and scarlet-gowned; he had a drawn, thin face, with large eyes and an aquiline nose; he spoke in a measured and careful way, as one might imagine a judge should, but the glances he gave around the court were quick and unpredictable. He looked at the accused, at the jury, then up at the public gallery, at counsel, at his notes—one never knew where he was going to look next, nor why he looked in any particular direction when he did. He picked up the knife with which a boy had been stabbed and killed; he pointed it towards the jury, he used it as a marker for his place among his notes, he put it aside again. It was a vicious knife, with a sharp point and a blade about six inches long, it shone brightly in his hand.

In the dock were two boys—the one who had actually done the stabbing, and another, his friend. When the latter was found not guilty by the jury his body gave a single convulsive shudder, and his head lolled forward: of all those I saw, he reacted most violently to what was said to him, and he was the one who was set free. A policeman touched his arm, and he was led away. Now the other boy stood alone in the dock.

He was, if I remember rightly, sixteen years and four months in age. He was wearing a dark blue suit: he was not tall for his age, but very heavily-built; he had a pale, ugly, putty-like face, thrust forward at the mouth, going back over the low brow to the dark hair brushed above. He moved heavily; he seemed sunk beneath feeling or knowing, in a kind of protective stupor.

According to witnesses, just before producing the knife with which he had stabbed the other boy he had shouted out, 'You think I'm nobody?' and now he really seemed like nobody: even the pity one felt for him became involuntarily a part of the movement of one's soul to dissociate oneself from him, to have nothing to do with him. He was found guilty of manslaughter, and was sentenced to five years' imprisonment: when he was taken beneath the court his head moved up and down in time with the movement of his feet, in a plodding, animal weariness and heaviness.

It was just by accident that I had come upon this case, with all its details of the argument in the lavatory, and the argument in the street outside, and the argument in the pub, and the fatal argument in the entrance to the dance-hall. No sooner had the boy left the dock than his place was taken by nine other youths, each of them charged on five separate counts of causing bodily harm to coloured people they had fallen on in the streets of Notting Hill—the very first series of incidents that led to what became known as the 'Notting Hill race riots'. The boy who had stood alone in the dock before the others came in had looked as though he might have done something low, unknowing, brutal. But these boys——!

'Guilty,' each of them said at first, as the charges were read out; and then one of them said, 'Guilty, sir,' and by the time the clerk had finished his roll, they were all saying, 'Guilty, sir,' like people anxious to learn the correct social usages for the company they found themselves in. There they were, the nine of them, five in the front row and four in the back; and what one felt throughout the trial was a kind of embarrassment that the evidence and the statements by prosecution and defence should have been about the youngsters before one. Embarrassment was stronger than pity, stronger than shame, stronger even than the sense of shock at what they had done. They were children—small, thin-wristed, thin-necked: there were only two of them that one could imagine being able to attack anyone bigger than a schoolboy in a playground. They were all quietly dressed, though not all wore ties and one had on an American-style checked shirt; they had the pinched, pale faces of English city boys—faces on which the lips and eyes look

vividly dark, everything else having no colour—and especially
in that courtroom, where the light came straight down from
above, through a flat, circular glass roof. Most of them were
seventeen years old; the oldest was twenty. You could have
seen them on a building lot, riding a delivery boy's bicycle,
being mate to an electrician: you wouldn't have looked twice.
There was nothing the least bit depraved, dissolute, or dangerous
about them. When they went below the court at an adjourn-
ment they looked through the glass for their relatives and
friends in the galleries, and discreetly but cheerfully waggled
their fingers at them, nodded their heads, smiled at the corners
of their mouths. They weren't sunken nobodies; they were
rather jaunty anybodies.

And that, really, was the most disturbing and frightening
thing about them. A couple of them, it was clear, were problems
in their work and with their families: there was one, aged
seventeen, who in his brief working career had already occupied
no less than eighteen different positions; and there was another
who had already had four larceny charges laid against him.
But those were the only two with troubled records of any kind.
For the rest, the detective-inspector in charge of the case had to
confirm defence counsel statements that this boy, and the other,
and the third, came from a good home, was regularly employed
at such-and-such-a-place, that his employers were satisfied with
him (many of the employers had said that they would gladly
take the boys back into their service), and that he had been
earning regular and quite substantial sums of money. The
highest paid among them was earning an average wage of ten
guineas a week; and they were all living at home. One of them
already owned a motor-car.

On a Saturday night about three weeks before, these boys
had been drinking at a pub (with the name, ironically enough,
of *The General Smuts*). They had then armed themselves, climbed
into the car owned by the one of them, and had gone on what
they described in their statements to the police as a 'nigger-
hunting expedition'. (It was recorded that the owner of the car
was the only one who had objected to the expedition—on the
grounds 'that there were too many of them to fit into the car'.)
The weapons with which they had armed themselves were

produced in court: they included four or five wooden staves, each three or four feet long, a car starter-handle, a knife, an air pistol, the leg of a table, and several iron railings with spear-shaped ends—the kind of railing one sees around London's parks and squares.

Their plan of action was very simple. They cruised around the streets of Notting Hill, and when they saw a solitary coloured man, all nine of them climbed out of the car and started beating him about the head and the body with the iron railings and staves; when their victim fell unconscious they left him bleeding on the pavement, climbed back into the car, and went on with their search. In this way they occupied themselves between the hours of about midnight and five in the morning. They never attacked groups, armed though they were: the biggest number they ever took on, the nine of them, was *two*, and that was on only one occasion. Of the people they attacked, three had had to be in hospital for a couple of weeks; through some lucky fluke none of the victims actually had his skull broken, though those that didn't manage to run away suffered severe scalp lacerations.

The depositions made by the accused were not read out in full to the court; but extracts were. Of the nine, only one in making his statement to the police seemed to have expressed any regret for what he had done; the others offered in mitigation merely such phrases as, 'Anyway, I hate niggers,' or, 'I whacked that nigger only a couple of times.' Their depositions sounded almost as brutal as their acts had been.

When defence counsel had made their pleas for their clients, the clerk called upon the accused to stand, and the judge began reading—very carefully—the speech which he had prepared. Before the judge was half-way through the speech one of the mothers at the back of the court had started to cry; when he passed sentence (and the length of the sentence was already headline-matter when I came out of the building) there was an indrawing of breath from every part of the court; a blonde woman struggled to her feet with a blind, wading movement of her arms, and was taken out in tears; then, as the sentences on the rest were read out, other women broke down. But the scenes weren't 'dramatic', as the papers were so quick to declare them; or if they were, they were dramatic in the confused, graceless way that most scenes really are, outside the newspapers. There was confusion on the benches where the relatives were sitting; there was confusion in the dock, where the prisoners turned to go, and then were halted because the proceedings weren't quite over yet. Then, suddenly, they had gone; and there was confusion outside the court, where the relatives gathered in little groups, none of them knowing what to do or where to go next. A very short man in a tight blue suit shook his finger at another and shouted, 'Four years! My boy's life is ruined. . . . You won't come into my house again . . .' and an embarrassed boy in a black leather lumberjacket took him by the arm and began pulling him away—'Come on, Dad, it doesn't help to carry on . . . it's no use, please come on, Dad.' Eventually the father, still gesticulating, allowed himself to be led away; and the others too dispersed. And the courts went on with their business. The judge who had tried the nine youths was now busy with five exceedingly distinguished-looking company directors and financial journalists, up on a charge of conspiring to defraud the public.

By their actions these nine youths had given notice that Notting Hill would be a good place to come to if one was looking for trouble; and the weekend following their attacks saw trouble— as we all know—on a very much bigger scale than anything the nine youths by themselves had been able to accomplish. The name 'Notting Hill' has been given to the riots, but the area in which disturbances of one kind or another took place—ranging from attacks on individual coloureds to the stoning of houses, attempts at arson, and street brawling on an extensive scale—is very wide indeed. It stretches from beyond the Edgware Road on the east to Shepherds Bush on the west; and from the Bayswater Road on the south to somewhere north of Westbourne Park. It includes the highly respectable—the almost Kensingtonian-squares and crescents of Holland Park; and the slums just to the north of Paddington where terraces of tall-windowed houses seem to show, as they peel hideously, the remains of every single coat of paint put on them since they were built a hundred years ago. The district is one that declines abruptly and improves again, as abruptly; and though some of the streets are like pits, with the houses standing bleakly on the pavements, or set back from the pavements only by railed and sunken areas where milk bottles and rubbish-bins accumulate, its overall air is not one of unspeakable and destructive poverty. Most of it, rather, is just grindingly dispirited and ugly, with an ugliness that too much of London shares for one to be shocked especially by it. And there are the bright new council housing estates.

Only around Westbourne Park—where the road humps itself over a little bridge, and acres of railway lines lie below to the west, towards Paddington—could one be really impressed by the number of coloured people there are in the streets. Only those few streets might remain in the mind as a place where the notion of a 'problem' might, under ordinary circumstances, occur to one. And though one can hardly measure the size of a problem by the number of people involved in it, it is worth repeating that out of a total population in Great Britain of something approaching fifty million, it is estimated that there are at most a few hundred thousand coloured people.

I must confess that much of my first reaction to the news of the disturbances was a feeling of sheer irritation and weariness—irritation particularly, because as a South African I couldn't help thinking immediately of what satisfaction and delight the news would give to the people one had opposed in South Africa; of the sanctimonious editorials that would be written and the self-satisfied speeches that would be made, on the lines of, '*Now* you won't be able to adopt superior moral attitudes to us; you see, you're even worse than we are . . .' et cetera, et cetera. And sure enough, that was the attitude of much of the South African press and many South African politicians; and at the time I felt I could hardly blame them for taking it. If the supposedly liberal, enlightened and law-abiding English failed to deal with *their* tiny colour-problem in terms other than those of violence and malevolence, what in heaven's name could one expect of a handful of Boers and their English-speaking fellow-whites scattered in isolation over the southern half of the African continent; what could one expect, for that matter, of the resentful and embittered southern whites in the United States?

Indeed, if hundreds of the English came out into the streets with their stones and milk-bottles and switch-knives because of the number of coloureds one sees in London, the wonder seemed to be that in a country like South Africa there is so much—not so little—of the rule of law.

For all the concern and generosity of spirit that was for the most part shown by the press, I found it impossible to be set at rest in any way by the discussions of the events and their causes that were held so lengthily and with such repetitiveness in all the English newspapers and periodicals. By now we must all have read a hundred times about white fears about housing, white sexual jealousy, white resentment of the habits of those West Indians who sit on pavements, or play guitars loudly, or live off a pittance in order to be able to buy a motor-car; just as we have read a hundred times that coloureds do *not* jump the queues for council housing, that very few of them live off immoral earnings or the peddling of drugs, that most of them are employed in hard jobs for a small reward, are anxious to live respectably, and have been driven to come to Great Britain because there is no work and no food for them in the West Indies. All these things are true; by now they have all been said, many times.

And they remain inadequate. Housing, or local employment practices, or the provision of welfare services do not either individually or collectively 'make up' the problem with which we are dealing now, which is, ultimately, a problem of feeling. To dodge that is something I do not believe we can afford to do: it is merely to try hopelessly to shove away from us what is in fact a part of our society—a deeper and more tenacious part than we are generally prepared to admit.

I don't want to dignify the meanness and vileness of racial prejudice by seeming to make of it something occult, pervasive, and inescapable. But it does seem to me that the nine boys who went into the streets of Notting Hill to stage their 'nigger hunt' —those nine boys with (mostly) good records, good jobs, and good homes—were prompted to do what they did by something much more difficult to deal with directly than a housing shortage; more difficult to deal with even than the psychological troubles they might have had in common with the anonymous boy whose trial preceded theirs. In their very viciousness and stupidity those nine boys showed themselves to be the victims of a complex of attitudes and beliefs which seem to be in the very bone and marrow of what we call 'our civilization'. The complex is equalled in its depth and tenacity only by that very different one with which Christian societies endlessly struggle in their relations with Jews.

What, after all, have the relations of 'White Civilization' (to use the necessarily crude South African term) hitherto been to the Negroes it now finds walking about in its streets? Historically, the relations of the white man to the black have been overwhelmingly those of slave-driver to slave, missionary to heathen, governor to tribesman, master to servant, superior to inferior. The white man until very recently has had to go out to meet the black man; and in doing so, at his most self-consciously noble, the white saw himself as a bringer of his 'civilization', with its order and system, to 'natives' whose lives would otherwise have been given over entirely (in the eyes of the white) to disorder, violence, and slovenliness. And at his least noble, of course, the white found in the powerlessness and poverty of black men nothing but an incitement to inflict as much degradation as he could upon them—the disorder which he imputed to 'black' life being as much of a temptation to the white as it ever was a threat. And this historical process—in itself bedevilling enough to the relations of white with black today—happened to meet and respond precisely with a kind of moral symbolism that was already there, as it were, in the structure of the white mind. Certainly it was in his language, and higher or deeper than the language we cannot go: like the air, we move within it. 'Black', it is perhaps necessary to remind ourselves, remains the colour of evil, of lies, of plague, of the murderer's heart, of the devil himself; and 'white'—white is purity and cleanliness and holiness, white is the raiment of the angels.

Do these things matter? How can they not? Recently, the American Negro writer, Ralph Ellison, commenting on the white American's 'fascination with the symbolism of blackness and whiteness', has remarked that the Negro, 'caught up in the negative side of this basic dualism', has been 'shackled' to almost everything the white folk-mind would repress from consciousness. 'The physical hardships and indignities of slavery,' Ellison goes on to say, 'were benign compared to this continuing debasement of our image. Because these things are bound up with their notions of chaos, it is impossible for many whites to consider questions of sex, women, economic opportunity, the national identity . . . without summoning malignant images of black men into consciousness.' Ellison is of course writing of the particular conditions of the United States; but what he has to say has its immediate relevance to the confrontation anywhere—whether in Johannesburg or Notting Hill—of white with black. And though the immigration of coloureds to Great Britain may be comparatively small and recent, the awareness of the possibilities and dangers of the confrontation has had a long time to sink deeply into the British national consciousness, through all the years that Britain exercised her imperial powers in the colonies.[1]

This may seem to have taken us a long way from the nine youths in the dock; I don't believe that it has. From what I saw of them it seemed to me that they—and presumably a great many of those who followed their example—felt themselves in some special and terrible way *permitted* to attack the coloureds who were their victims; and that in their attitudes to what they did (and in the attitudes of their parents to them and the court) there was an element of something approaching self-righteousness, which would have been absent had their victims belonged to some other group, or merely to another gang. These young men were trapped within a history; being both weak and violent, they could not escape from it—no more than in the event they could escape from the consequences of those religious beliefs of ours which declare every man to be equal before God, or those secular ambitions of ours which struggle to see every man as an equal before the law.

And surely it was in response to this unspoken yet suspected notion of 'permittedness' that such exceptionally heavy sentences were passed, and were so heartily approved of by practically every section of British public opinion.

[1] I give another, and a later, view of this kind of speculation in the essay entitled *James Baldwin and the American Negro*.

The balance of aggression and restraint is never struck, but societies, like people, live as well as they can by trying for it.

There is one other 'underground' aspect of the public reaction to the riots which has not, so far as I know, been referred to anywhere. It is an aspect that it is curiously difficult to write about—for two paradoxical reasons: on the one hand it may appear flippant and tasteless to mention it at all, and on the other hand the issues it raises are far too large to be dealt with in the context of the riots themselves. What I am referring to here is the fact that on the part of a great many articulate and liberal-minded people the major response to the riots was one of a studied and deliberate indifference.

I was prepared to ascribe my own reaction of 'weariness' to my being a South African; but I was surprised to find that so very many other people who weren't South Africans seemed to be equally weary. This is something one would never guess from reading the newspapers; but unless the people I happen to have met have been untypical to an inexplicable degree, this is the truth of their reaction. People didn't want to read about the riots; they didn't want to hear about the riots; they wanted as little as they possibly could to do with the riots—even in the way of speculation and conversation, and least of all in any way that might involve their emotions directly. Time after time I encountered this reaction among people whom one ordinarily would have expected to have been concerned with public events and affairs of the day. Often people seemed ashamed of their indifference, and apologized for it, but by and large they were true to it nevertheless.

The truth is that the English liberals are bored, bored, bored; Notting Hill showed up once again how thoroughly bored the English liberals are with their own liberalism. (I am of course using the word as it is used in the United States and South Africa, in a sense that has nothing to do with party-politics.) And—setting aside all the other reasons there are for a sense of sheer exhaustion with public affairs—how can the liberals in England *not* be bored, when their words have had such a devastating triumph? We are all liberals nowadays: when we speak, at any rate, no matter what we may feel, and not only in

England. What liberal can take exception to the words in which
that well-known liberal, Mr Krushchev, presents his pleas,
dicta, ultimata? Is there a South American dictator who does
not announce his intentions in terms of free speech, universal
suffrage, equality before the law, and a minimum standard of
living? Or a Middle Eastern potentate? Dr Verwoerd will roar
you democracy as gently as any sucking dove—let alone Messrs
Macmillan and Gaitskell, Eisenhower and De Gaulle. Even the
out-and-out Fascists—the Mosleyites and the League of
Empire Loyalists and suchlike—have taken to speaking in the
accents of concern, enlightenment, and consideration. *Keep
Britain White* they scrawl on brick walls; but in their literature
they will fervently assure you that they feel very sorry for the
West Indians; that they think it shocking that West Indians
should be discriminated against in housing or employment or
socially; and that that is one of the main reasons why they
implore the government to keep them out of the country. And
if—alongside these generous and high-minded avowals—they
print details of the number of coloureds charged with sexual
offences, they will be quick to point out that they feel it is their
duty to keep the public informed—just as they are quick to
claim that they are doing no more than exercise the democratic
rights they respect so much when they move into a troubled
area like Notting Hill with their platforms, loudspeakers and
Union Jacks.

And so it goes. The liberal hears his own words, distorted and
magnified, coming from the lips of people he distrusts and
despises. And he conceives a disgust for his own words. He never
hears any words but his own; and yet when he looks around he
sees that under the words of fairness, kindness and tolerance,
there breed unchecked all the old rancours and hatreds and
meannesses; all the old lusts for violence. So he turns away,
stops his ears altogether, talks about something else.

I happen to believe that there is an element of health in this
turning away; that 'apathy' is a political weapon that the
authoritarian bullies of all kinds are finding it hard to turn to
their own purposes; that fatigue and indifference in a time like
the present can be positively restorative. But the one thing we
cannot afford to be indifferent about is our sense of fact. If we

retain our sense of fact, our words might yet regain their meanings.

Many well-intentioned people have said, 'At least these disturbances have made everybody wake up, and that's a good thing; no one can say now that the problem doesn't exist.' I think that this is a mistake: I don't believe that there is anything 'good'—even by way of warning—about what has happened. Peace breeds peace; but violence breeds violence and anger breeds anger; and to know that a man is hated—to read in the papers, see on the streets, hear on buses that a man is hated—makes others hate him more than before, not less so. There is a perverse logic about the way these things move; and so far from the riots in Notting Hill and Nottingham having 'released' a charge of tension, I am convinced that in fact they have merely exacerbated what tensions there were before.

Does this mean we may expect more outbreaks of the kind that have recently taken place? Probably it does. But the British (despite the hopes of some South African politicians) *are* tolerant and law-abiding and gentle, and the forces making for peace are immeasurably stronger than those making for repeated disorder of a large-scale kind. But what has happened will almost certainly mean more insults and gibes being flung at individual West Indians, more isolated incidents of violence, more landladies refusing to let accommodation to coloured people. The problem is a tough and bitter one; and it is going to be with us for a long time. It does seem to me that a true and undiscouraged acknowledgement of its toughness is a first and necessary part of dealing with it.

1958

PLAGUE SPOT

He had no future. He disdained it. . . . His thoughts caressed the images of ruin and destruction. He walked frail, insignificant, shabby, miserable—and terrible in the simplicity of his idea calling madness and despair to the regeneration of the world. Nobody looked at him. He passed on, unsuspected and deadly, like a pest in the street full of men.
                                   Joseph Conrad: *The Secret Agent.*

ONE MUST KEEP IT in proportion: it was a miserable, back-street affair, involving at most a couple of hundred people. And as for the violence of it—after all, I stood, a Jew, among a crowd who were yelling 'F——ing Jews!' almost as often as they opened their mouths, and I felt no personal fear at all, as I would certainly have done among a crowd uttering similar sentiments in my native South Africa. And when people began rocking a car and beating on it with their fists, and when some of them were arrested, there was a great deal of shouting, fist-waving, spitting, but no truncheons were drawn, no blood was spilt, and traffic passed without hindrance just at the end of the block, barely thirty yards away.

'They have tried to make Notting Hill a dirty word,' Mosley cried at one point: looking at the man it was impossible to forget that the life-work of his friends and exemplars had been to make of Europe a dirty word—to make of it a stinking pit, an abattoir. And now he stood there, still alive, speaking through a loudspeaker, a parliamentary candidate for the constituency of North Kensington. He had passed close by me, on his way to the van which he mounted to make his speech; almost the first thing I had seen of him was the gum above his upper teeth, a

64

livid, almost orange colour, as he lifted his lip in a smile. Then
he was up above, one hand lifted to acknowledge the cheers (and
the few boos) with which he was greeted. He was, at first,
pitiful, with his freckled forehead, his bad teeth, and his portly
aristocratic air of the man of affairs, which merely drew one's
attention to the miserable failure his life has been: he was
simply too old still to be climbing on to the backs of open trucks
in sordid streets to make his speeches. And when he opened his
speech by telling the crowd that the television cameras of the
Columbia Broadcasting System were present he spoke as if he
mentioned this only to flatter his audience, to help build up its
own estimation of itself. Yet, unmistakably, at the end of his
public life, it was his own estimation of himself that was being
built up by the presence of the cameras of what he proudly
announced to be 'the second-largest radio and television network
in the world'.

I had been waiting for a long time for Mosley to come—he
was very late—and after listening to him for about ten minutes,
I left, to find a place where I could have a cup of tea; I knew he
would still be there when I returned. Previously I had been
listening, while waiting, to one of Mosley's lieutenants, a bent-
nosed, youngish man, in a baggy sports jacket, who had seemed
to hang loosely behind his own magnified voice. Nothing that
Mosley said in the first ten minutes of his speech I had not
already heard from the young man. There was one issue, and
one issue only, on which Mosley was fighting the election: the
Negroes. 'Get them off our backs,' the young man cried;
'Deport them—in a humane, British way,' Mosley said more
urbanely: but the crowd wasn't fooled for a moment by his
urbanity, or by his humanity. 'Dirty niggers! F——ing Spades!
Baboons, baboons, baboons!' they cried in support, and Mosley
lifted his hand to acknowledge their fervour. There were no
West Indians in the crowd, or if there were, they were at its very
outskirts; previously, several had passed through the crowd,
without any of them being molested in any way. Interrupters
were, however, very promptly silenced by the volume of noise
produced by Mosley's supporters, who cried at them: 'Jew-boy!
Israel! F——ing Jew!' In point of fact, I would say that none of
the few hecklers were actually Jewish (the meeting happened to

c

be taking place on the Jewish New Year's Day); but the crowd wasn't capable of making discriminations among those it considered to be its enemies.

Of some of Mosley's supporters one can say that they wore their hatreds, their sicknesses, like badges on their flesh; I recall one creature who could not keep his head still for a moment, nor any feature on it, so that while his head nodded and trembled, his eyes blinked, his lips twitched, even his nose moved. And then there was a woman with a square body in a red flowered dress; her upper lip, painted to match her dress, was extraordinarily long and came to a point in the middle, like a beak, while above, grotesquely, were stretched a pair of wide gaping nostrils. And both the twitcher and that woman, so ugly one looked at them and looked away, were obviously receiving solace from the knowledge that there was one man in the world who spoke directly to the horror their lives were, and would make that same horror of the whole world, if he could. Yet there were also ordinary-looking working-class youths in Italianate clothes and elaborate hair-styles; a smartly-dressed woman in navy blue with high colour in her cheeks; an elderly gentleman with a brimless sports-car cap, a military moustache, and a trim regimental or club blazer, who could have been anybody's neighbour in any middle-class area. And they all cheered, listened, they all hated alike.

I left them, as I have said, and returned about thirty minutes later, just in time for Mosley's peroration. Now he was no longer pitiful, not because his audience had grown; not because he seemed any more of a threat than he had been before; but because it is impossible to pity a man who is where he most wants to be. And Mosley was there: in the blank, glazed world of the demagogue, where all distinction between himself and the world-not-himself was lost. When he prophesied victory for himself he was speaking the truth; for he had already conquered. In that narrow street, black and yellow with filth and sunlight, he heard only his own voice, magnified and trapped between brick walls; he *was* his voice, and his voice filled all the space he was conscious of. He came to his climax, he ceased, and the cheers (and the booing from a section of the crowd standing towards the back) broke out anew.

The questions that followed seemed to have been planted. Would Mosley clear up the black brothels? Yes, he would clear up the black brothels. Would Mosley protect the rights of all white tenants? Yes, he would protect the rights of all white tenants. Would Mosley investigate why the police were protecting the black 'vice-kings'? Mosley replied that the police were a fine body of men, 'as British as we are', and it was the corrupt politicians who gave them their orders who had to be cleared out of office. The police listened stolidly, expressionlessly: there were a great many of them scattered about, including two senior officers, and throughout they had been moving among the crowd, coming between hecklers and Mosley's supporters, standing with folded arms behind those who screamed most loudly, consulting together and moving off again in pairs. Mosley was anxious not to offend them; but the crowd cared less, as one soon saw when the trouble began.

The 'trouble' came in the form of a Labour Party loudspeaker car, which began to make its way through the crowd—an act which I have no doubt at all was intended to be provocative, and which succeeded in being so. Mosley had come to his climax, in his speech; but what of his supporters, who had been screaming their violence and imprecations into the air, and were now suddenly to be abandoned, each one of them alone again in a world that was as huge and indifferent to them as it had ever been? No wonder they dreaded their awakening; no wonder they rushed at the Labour Party car and began rocking it and beating at it with their fists, cursing, raving, saved for the moment. And no wonder that the police, after their afternoon of boredom and tension, suddenly unleashed their own violence. With faces as pale and eyes as dark as those of the mob, they lunged, they grabbed, they had one youth, and a second, and were dragging them off to the Black Maria parked discreetly down the block; they grabbed a third, older man and he too was carried in a bunch of policemen and others down the street. By that time the car was through, though someone seemed to have slashed at it as it went past, for at the end of the block it halted, one tyre collapsed around the wheel-hub. In tears, the wife and the three little daughters of the last man to be arrested were trying to get into the Black Maria, but they were held back;

when the van drove away, leaving them in the street, one of the little girls screamed, 'Isn't Daddy coming back?'

A few policemen stood guard over the Labour Party car, but by this time most of the mob seemed to have forgotten all about it: their hatred was turned altogether against the police. 'F——ing rozzers! They nick our boys and let the Spades go! The Spades pay them for the job! Nigger-lovers! Let the boys go! Let the boys go!' They shouted and waved their fists; but they kept their distance. The mother and three little girls were put into a car and driven away; when I turned I saw that Mosley had gone. The meeting, the incident, such as it was, was over; though a smaller crowd was gathering hostilely now around a Liberal Party car which had just arrived on the scene. 'Jew-boy!' they cried at the Liberal candidate. 'Jew-boy!' The twitching man scurried past me. 'Baboons!' he was saying to himself. Still the crowd milled in the street, but soon each member of it would have to go, on his own, down other streets.

1959

THE EAST END

IN 1902, ON HIS way to South Africa, my father, who was then a boy of sixteen, spent several weeks in the East End of London, living in the house of a woman who came from the same *shtetl* as himself in Latvia. Of these weeks my father remembered chiefly the drunken men and women lying on the pavements outside the pubs on Friday evenings, and his own attempts to pay for his keep by hiring a barrow and peddling pots and pans from it. The attempt was a miserable failure; in the end, he did not manage to earn enough to cover the cost of hiring the barrow, let alone the cost of his board and lodging. And he got lost innumerable times; on one such occasion he gratefully stumbled into a mission for converting the Jews, where they gave him bread and cocoa, and where he found Yiddish newspapers to read. Subsequently, he returned many times to that mission, for the sake of the bread, cocoa and newspapers; but never, he would scornfully insist, for the sake of the gospel.

About fifty years later I went with him down Whitechapel Road to the house in Mile End Road in which he had boarded. The house was still standing; but all around it was a wasteland, where the bombs had fallen. This was the first time I had been to the East End; and the district seemed to me empty, dusty and featureless, much like any other in London, except for the extent of the bomb-damage. Whatever the East End might have been in my father's day, it seemed clear that it was that no longer. Later, I went back three or four times on my own, for various reasons, but, wandering up and down the Whitechapel Road, saw little to detain me, little to rouse my interest, little that made me feel I had any connection with the place, either as the son of my father or simply as a sightseer, a newcomer to London.

It seems to me extraordinary now that I should have been so wrong: how wrong I was shown in the course of a single visit paid to the East End in the company of a friend who was born there and still lives there, and who was able to point out to me just how much I had missed previously. However, though I now believe I was altogether mistaken in finding the East End featureless and commonplace before, I can still, in a way, see exactly why I found it so. The shop-windows of the East End are filled with the kind of goods one sees in shop-windows anywhere else, its main streets are crowded with lorries grinding their way through traffic as heavy and noisy as any other in London, its people for the most part wear the clothes that other Londoners wear, they buy the same newspapers from vendors on street corners and the same huge hoardings stare down at them from walls. If I were to give the impression that the East End, as I saw it on a sunny summer's afternoon a few months ago, is in any way isolated from the London of today, then I would be falsifying what it is, and (I should imagine) what it always has been. The fact is that the presence everywhere of so much which is commonplace and unremarkable in the East End makes the survival of its intense, half-secret differentness all the more remarkable, not less so.

Once one's eyes have been opened, one can distinguish precisely each of the historical layers within the East End; one can see how each era succeeded that previous to it, and how they all yet continue to coexist with one another in a simultaneity that surprises one at almost every corner. There are a few eighteenth-century houses and shop-fronts still standing— superbly elegant in design, ruinous in condition. Succeeding these in time, and overwhelming them in terms of space occupied, are the buildings of the Victorian era, varying in size from huge black warehouses and even more forbidding multi-storeyed tenements to shrunken terraces on both sides of lanes a few paces wide. Then there are all the signs of the great Jewish influx from about 1880 on; and, lastly, there is the new or incipient ghetto of Pakistanis and West Indians, Pakistanis chiefly. The inhabitants of both these ghettoes, of course, simply took possession of the houses built by the previous tenants of the area, whose own descendants also continued to live there. And, interpenetrating with all the above are a host of other layers, of signs of other historical events or immigrations. There are the LCC housing estates built since the war, the houses of Swedish merchants in Swedenborg Square, a tiny Maltese enclave (including the head-quarters of the 'Maltese Liberal Party'), an abandoned mission for German seamen, Hugenot place-names in Spitalfields, doss-houses, homes for fallen women, bomb-sites in which the rubbish of twenty years has accumulated.

All these can be dated, more or less: this earlier than that, that later than that. But they stand adjacent to one another, and are used indifferently by the people who throng in the streets, and who are themselves a kind of compendium of the area's history. I suppose the people, too, can be divided into four main categories—there are the Jews, the English, the Pakistanis, and the deadbeats. As for the latter, one can hardly describe them as Dickensian; one has to reach farther back for a word to describe them, farther even than Shakespeare ('Poor Tom's a-cold')—they are positively medieval in the intensity of their decrepitude, and medieval also just in their sheer numbers. There are dozens of them, both men and women; of the men I remember particularly one indignant, gesticulating starveling dressed entirely, so far as I could make out, in a tattered army greatcoat and a bristle of beard; and an elephantine, blank-faced, bald-headed creature sitting in the sun with his eyes closed and his trousers burst wide open. His hat was between his feet, and in his hat was half a loaf of bread. Just as the junk-yards and bomb-sites are filled with the oiliest, dustiest, most unusable rubbish imaginable, so the deadbeats of the East End seem more beat than any others in London.

And one catches stray glimpses of so many other sorts of people—West Indians sprawling full-length on benches in tiny cafés, with the radio blaring rock-and-roll; two Italian women talking excitedly over a wall; a small boy wheeling a pram with *two* fat, fair-haired babies lolling inside it; workmen lounging in the sun on the loading-platforms of the warehouses; un-identifiable hoodlums hanging around 'clubs' one could identify at a glance. And, again and again, the Pakistanis standing in

the doors of their shops, and—for me, most remarkable of all—
the Jews in the doors of theirs.

These alleyways of shops are so intimate and so remote they are
like something I might have seen in one of my own dreams.
Déjà vu is hardly the word for the sensation they arouse; it is
more physical than anything else, as though a garment has been
slipped over me, which fits me perfectly and yet muffles and
confines me. And it is curious that it should seem to me that I
have known this sensation many times before, when in fact I've
seen such streets only twice in my entire life: once when I was
driving with a friend through New York's Lower East Side, and
he turned off Delancey Street into a side-street; and the second
time now, in Stepney.

What, I wanted to ask aloud, are they doing, what are the
Jews still doing here? How can they still be here? It's all
supposed to be over, it's supposed to be finished and done with,
this style of life in streets of this kind. Don't these Jews know it?
Surely they just can't go on and on, as though nothing has
changed, as though there's been no war (no First World War,
let alone Second), no Hitler, no bombing, no State of Israel, no
migration to the northern suburbs, no rise into the professional
class, no men in space. But apparently they do go on, doing the
same things, carrying on the same trades, that they were busy
with when my father pushed his hired barrow through these
streets. They are in the garment trade: piece-goods converters,
dress trimmers, button and buckle manufacturers, shirt
specialists, pressers and renovators, furriers and skin merchants,
manufacturers of bias bindings. They are in the food trade,
selling chicken and kosher salamis, pickled cucumbers, salt
beef, *halvah*, horseradish, three-course kosher meals for 4/6d.
They stand beside barrows laden with second-hand clothes or
South African fruit; they bicker outside betting-shops; they run
tiny printing-houses; in one narrow alley there are no less than
half a dozen Jewish jewellers' shops.

We passed behind Petticoat Lane; and, passing behind it, I
realized again just how little of the Jewish East End I had seen
on my previous visits, when I had walked dutifully up and down
the Lane. I had come there, like everyone else, because Petti-

coat Lane is shabby, exotic and colourful. But Petticoat Lane *knows* it's exotic and colourful; whereas the far more shabby streets behind it and below it are innocent in a way, self-absorbed, sunk so deeply into themselves that you feel nothing could ever pull them up into self-consciousness. They are devoid of any obvious colour or exoticism; instead, they are filled with something much more difficult to describe, a kind of stillness or repose which the noise and traffic around them seem powerless to disturb, and which the activity of the people within these lanes could only make more intense.

So, down the alleys, in basement rooms and upstairs, groups of women work away at their sewing machines; in the gutters rags thrown out from the workshops accumulate in multi-coloured piles; in the shops men sit and talk to one another or stand in their doorways with their thumbs in their trouser-tops, looking a few yards across the cobbles, littered with cabbage-leaves and wood-shavings, to shops as small as their own; women lean their bosoms on their barrows and eye their own goods; on chairs put out in the sun old *bobbes* doze and start awake and at last fall deeply asleep; again you hear a whirr and a chatter of machines and you pass another little tucked-away sweatshop. There seem to be no Jewish children about, and the men and women are all middle-aged or older—the women generally plump, the men unshaven, waistcoated, wearing their hats on the backs of their heads. And in between are the Pakistanis in their own shops with their own smells, sometimes rows of such shops, succeeding or facing a row of Jewish shops; there are the women from the LCC estates, carrying their shopping-bags in their hands; a solitary Negro sitting on an upended barrel in the middle of a bomb-site; the incisive blaze and tumult of a main street; then yet another sunken lane of stillness.

There seemed to be six or eight lanes where the stillness (as I've called it; though it was the noisiest, most animated stillness imaginable) was especially noticeable; where the old life seemed to be continuing itself so fully, in such vivid familiar detail, that one could hardly think of it as a continuation—it seemed more a standing motionless, a suspension of time and change. But even in these streets there was a stillness of another kind, too; a stillness of abandonment and dislocation; of empty

C*

premises and blind shop-windows; of faded names of people who had long since left and businesses no longer active; of the forlorn, pockmarked, never-to-be-renewed Yiddish signs flaking from the walls on which they had been painted. My friend kept saying to me, 'You should have seen it ten years ago,' and I'm sure he was right, I'm sure that over the last ten years the area has been denuded of the Jews who gave it so much of its characteristic life. And yet I'm just as sure that ten years ago people were saying, 'You should have seen it ten years ago, before the bombing,' and that ten years before they had said the same thing again. And it was almost impossible to believe, standing in one of those still lanes, that in ten years' time one wouldn't be able to say, in front of the same shops, with the same kind of people looking over the same barrows, with the same smell in one's nostrils, 'Ah, but you should have seen it ten years ago!' It is unimaginable that that life should disappear; or, rather, it was unimaginable for me, then, seeing it for the first time, and realizing that I had believed it had already disappeared completely, years ago, wars ago, generations ago.

But the last Yiddish theatre is now a Bingo Hall. And most of the Jewish bookshops were pitiful. My guide pointed out to me how remarkable it was that in one slum street, which had always been a slum street, there should have been no less than five bookshops—how much that reveals of the inclinations and ambitions of the Jews who lived in Whitechapel. But three of the five in that street were hopelessly bare, and the few books in them (printed in Cracow, in Dresden, in New York, in Warsaw) were covered in black grime. These shops also offered for sale *tallithim* and *tallith*-bags and *menorot*, and hideously printed cloths showing vistas of Jerusalem, or pictures of skull-capped, earlocked boys at prayer, watched over by benign rabbis. But they sold few enough of these, to judge by how dusty they were, and how much space on the shelves and in the windows each article had to itself. One of the shops, however, did seem to be well-stocked, and was full of men conversing loudly with one another; they looked as though they had been talking there all day.

Three or four of the synagogues I saw were not rundown; they were poor, but had obviously been maintained with devotion, and seemed to be in daily use. And two of them, at least, were in conspicuously handsome buildings; I was told that they had almost certainly once been Methodist or Baptist chapels, which had been taken over by the Jews and used by them ever since. Will they become mosques, eventually? It is hardly possible to see any other end for them. And one tiny synagogue, the size of a room, the height of a man, at the end of a small, sunless cul-de-sac, had actually been abandoned; its doors had been replaced with corrugated iron, and the Hebrew lettering cut out in metal over the lintel was the only sign to show what it once had been.

An elegaic note is almost unavoidable in talking about the Jewish East End; but what I've been anxious to do here is simply to record my astonishment, as a newcomer, at finding it still so very much alive. And when one looks at the bewildering variety of people who walk about the East End's streets, who lean against its walls, who sit on its pavements, who shout at one another from its upstairs windows, one realizes that the decline of one community means, after all, little more than the rise of another; and that none disappears entirely. One can't help thinking of this as a kind of victory, today; and one shouldn't allow oneself to be dissuaded from doing so by the humble, human, enduring squalor of the way it has been won.

1962

Part Two

SOUTHERN AFRICA

SOUTH AFRICA:

Explanations and Speculations

THOUGH MY LATEST RETURN to South Africa happened to coincide (quite unintentionally) with the Sharpeville crisis, my single overwhelming impression of South Africa, when I look back now, is not political. What I chiefly remember of the country are its spaces, simply; all the empty unused landscapes of a country that still seems to lie bereft of any human past, untouched by its own history. Blue sky, brown earth, and people who live unaccommodated between: that is the abiding image of South Africa. There is something remote, far-sunken about the country, dwarfing the people who live in it, and making them, in turn, seem remote from one another. Divided and self-divided again, they live: the English-speaking whites, the Afrikaans-speaking whites, the black-skinned peoples, speaking a multitude of their own languages. Yet, strangely, it wasn't the Blacks who seemed most remote to me this time, but the Afrikaners, the Boers, who claim, of all South Africans, to be most truly South African. If they are, it is because, in a lost country, they are most lost: a people with a past they cannot recognize for what it was, a present that is hateful to them, and no future at all.

The trains cross and re-cross the Karroo, where the gaunt *koppies* stand out of the veld, littered untidily with boulders, as if the gods who had made them could not be bothered to clean up the mess of their own materials; alongside the railway track there runs the clean blue National Road, and at intervals a moving car glitters on it, travelling faster than the train, yet

79

seeming to make no progress at all against the spaces of earth
and sky beyond. Then one comes to a tiny bleached station; the
train waits for another train, or for nothing, and moves on
again, north or south. North lies Johannesburg and the gold
mines, with all their shining dumps among the suburbs; south-
wards is Cape Town, 'the fairest Cape we saw in our circum-
navigation of the globe', as Sir Francis Drake described it—
still fair, too, classically so, with the mountains to one side and
the sea to the other, and borders of golden sand between. But
how far apart from one another these cities are, what silences
lie between them!

Space, then, is vivid in the memory; and so too, unexpectedly,
is poverty. Of course, the poverty of the blacks was expected;
and yet it came as a shock, it is so much uglier and more de-
graded than one could truly recollect, living in a country like
England. But this is not the only kind of poverty one sees in
South Africa; there are poor white people too, and one sees
their miserable houses everywhere: corrugated iron above, tiny
stoeps in front, a linoleum bareness indoors. The people who live
in these houses occupy menial positions, they earn miserable
wages, they clamour for credit at the end of each month from
their local Indian trader. True, they are far better-off than the
Africans; true, they are better-off than they themselves have
ever been in their own history. Yet they remain poor, threatened
people, almost entirely Afrikaans-speaking; there are tens of
thousands of them, living in every town and *dorp* in the country.

How easy it would be, seeing the islands of population and
poverty in the great emptiness of the country, to imagine South
Africa squalid, stagnating, ignored, as it was through most of
the nineteenth century. But they found diamonds, they struck
gold! Then, and only then, did that sad, unattractive outpost,
which had previously drawn fewer immigrants than Australia
or New Zealand, call urgently to Cornish miners and Lithuanian
Jews; then the African tribesmen began streaming to the cities,
which only then began to grow. Now South Africa supplies
half the world's gold and half the world's diamonds; it exports
uranium and manganese, fruit and fish and wool, boots and
blankets. Stark on the veld the cities grew, and still grow:
cities of apartment houses and department stores, private

swimming pools and parking problems. The trains and planes
run on time; the radio advertises Drene shampoo and Pepsodent
toothpaste; the newspapers appear and are avidly read; the
factories send their smoke into the air; the universities do re-
search into the origins of heart-disease. (Why, why are the
Africans so much less prone to heart-disease than the whites?)
Crudity still marks the manners of the people, black and white
alike, still marks even their faces; but who could be surprised
to find so recently developed a country crude, bare and pro-
vincial? And if the cities are still small by European or American
standards, it must be remembered that half the cities' popula-
tions travel in to do their work, and travel out again miles, to
the shadow-cities that lie around every named city. From his
trains the white man sees these shadow-cities: rows of small
barrack-buildings, marching across the sides of barren nameless
hills.

The contrasts of silence and noise, isolation and busyness,
poverty and wealth, are in themselves bewildering; and yet at
the same time they help to make plain the nature of the
conflicts which rack the country.

The English-speaking—that is, those who are of English descent,
and the Jews who are associated with them—still own the
cities, by and large; they own the mines, the factories, the
department stores, the homes in the expensive suburbs. For the
sake of the mines, the English fought the Boers, in the Anglo-
Boer War at the beginning of this century, and defeated them.
After the Boers had been defeated, the English were magnanimous to them, and gave them self-government; but the English
kept the mines and were contemptuous of the people to whom
they had been so magnanimous. The English now are a minority
among the whites, and have no political power, or prospect of
achieving political power once again; but they retain in their
hands most of the wealth of the country. And though they
themselves hardly know it, they retain too something of a
pragmatic, self-seeking and hence self-saving temperateness that
seems to have come to them with their language, and with as
little effort as their language. Individual English South Africans
may loathe the blacks as heartily as individual Afrikaners; but

as a group, the English-speaking would, I am convinced, make some attempt to compromise with the blacks, while there is still time.

But politically they are powerless. Power is in the hands of the Nationalist Afrikaners; and with them the case is entirely different. Who can describe an unknown people in a paragraph? It is better perhaps not to make the attempt, especially when the people is as complex and as psychologically riven as the Afrikaners. All one can ask is that the attempt be made to imagine a European people who settled in a strange land, at the foot of a remote continent, and who then trekked away into the interior—trekked away not only in search of better lands and wider pastures, but fleeing, always, from the dominance of Europe. Even when 'Europe' was the Holland they came from, they resented it; when 'Europe' became an alien England, they redoubled their efforts to get away from it. Significantly, their language ceased to be Dutch and became Afrikaans, a language that Hollanders now have difficulty in following; and what happened to their language happened too to many of the other laws and institutions which they had brought with them. Even their Christianity seemed to become more an Old Testament than a New Testament creed; and in the image of the Chosen People, wandering among the heathen in the wilderness, the Afrikaners saw themselves.

The heathen were the blacks, whom the Boers met as they moved forward, and whom they fought and fought again, and conquered. Then, in the interior of the country, they established their two Republics. And by a cruel and malignant irony (as it still seems to many of them) they established their pastoral republics right on top of the diamond and gold fields. The diamond fields were taken away from them easily, by the British; the gold fields were more difficult to filch, and a war had to be fought before the Boers were broken and the investors in London felt their money to be safe. And the British broke the Boers again, when the war was over, by their contempt: the contempt of the victor for the vanquished, of the rich for the poor, of the metropolitan for the colonial, of the townee for the 'backvelder', of the man who spoke English for the man who spoke an un-recognized and (at that time) unwritten *taal*. Contempt was

worse than war, turned defeat into rancour, persisting from generation to generation. And to this day the background of the Afrikaner Nationalist movement has remained an unquestioned enmity towards the blacks, a deep sense of grievance towards the English, and an immense sensitivity to insult.

And what of the Africans, outnumbering by three or four to one both the English- and Afrikaans-speaking whites? In the Reserves a kind of semi-tribal life still persists, and the tourists can see the women grinding corn and making beer. But the young men are absent, away in the cities, and though they come to the cities empty-handed they bring with them qualities that are the secret envy and wonder of every white man: a quickness and fullness of laughter, a litheness of limb, an ability to endure discomfort that is as much an attitude of the mind as a strength of the body. But they come, too, it must be added, pitifully ignorant of the skills they need to wage successfully a political and social struggle like the one in which, willy-nilly, they have been thrust: they come illiterate, they come ignorant of the most rudimentary technical knowledge, they come divided among themselves. Leaders are emerging, the knowledge is being acquired; but about the mass one must say that only a people shorn of their own history would have been so slow in formulating a national ideal for which to struggle; and only a people so poor that they can in some measure be contented with, or even count as riches, their wages and possessions in the great city slums, would ever have tolerated the conditions under which they live. One can say too that only a people who have never learned to handle firearms or explosives would hitherto have offered so little effective fight against their own servitude.

Consider what has been given as the background of the Afrikaner in relation to the English: the Afrikaner has suffered defeat, dispossession, and contumely. Then consider what, in a more severe degree, the black man has suffered at the hands of the white: defeat, dispossession and contumely. Consider too that the Afrikaners have hitherto been primarily a pastoral people, only now being drawn into the cities: is this not true, too, of the Africans? Afrikaner and African alike remember their defeats with bitterness; alike they are frightened and confused by their own emergence into cities that belong always to others; alike they hunger with an unceasing hunger for the goods and glories of these same cities: the fish-and-chip shops, the Coca-Cola girls with naked legs twenty feet high, the great pneumatic cars, the cinemas, the houses with private swimming pools. (The full-fed intellectuals of Great Britain and the United States may already have turned away in disgust from these things; but for others, who come from the isolation and poverty I have described, the products of the factories and assembly plants are the wonders of the world. And if, in their fastidiousness, the intellectuals of Britain and the United States should ever forget this, they will show themselves to be unthinking and irresponsible fools. In this context South Africa is but a single instance of a universal truth.)

Of course, to return to the comparison between the Africans and the Afrikaners, there are immense differences between the two groups. Whatever the disadvantages he has suffered, *vis-à-vis* the English, the Afrikaner has had every advantage over the black. The Afrikaner has always ruled over the African, he has always been literate, he has always had a say in the government over him: in a word, he has always had a white skin. Yet the parallel between the two groups remains true and close enough to both African and Afrikaner for each to hate the reflection of himself he sees in the other's features. There is no peace for them, no common cause, in the similitude, that's for sure.

And yet—over the last few decades, and certainly since the beginning of the Second World War, South Africa has become steadily wealthier and wealthier. The 'poor whites', as a class, have all but disappeared, though many whites remain comparatively poor; the Afrikaans farmers are generally prosperous; the Afrikaans share in the commerce and industry of the country, though still very small, is growing with every year that passes. At the same time, the earnings of the blacks have risen even faster, proportionately, than the earnings of the whites—though they remain deplorably low—and a tiny African middle-class has begun to emerge. For this reason there is a deep reluctance on the part of many Africans to risk what they have in an all-out political war against the whites; and for this reason, too, it is just possible that the Afrikaners, on their side, might be prepared to make concessions that would have been unthinkable to them only a few years ago. The more they share in it, the more the Afrikaners value the prosperity of the country, which can be sustained only by peace.

And not only has the Afrikaner grown more prosperous; by their repeated political victories over the 'English' opposition, the Afrikaner Nationalists have managed to assuage something of their own rankling sense of defeat and injury. Materially and psychologically, the Afrikaner has a greater stake than ever before in the well-being of the country.

This is perhaps the strangest truth about South Africa: *if* the Afrikaner will make concessions, it is because he now has more to lose, not less, than ever before in his history.

But which, for the Nationalist Afrikaner, is stronger: the voice of his own material hopes for himself, or all the embittered and enraged voices of his own past? Does he want to build more than he wants to destroy? Does he want to live more than he wants to die? At the moment, it is certain, he wants to do both: to build and to destroy; to live and to die.

Death for him has many attractions, and he gives it his dearest names: 'the purity of the race', 'the destiny of the *volk*', 'white civilization', '*baasskap*' (boss-hood). But under these names of life, there lurks the will to war and destruction: destruction of the enemy and the self alike. Why, until very recently, should the Afrikaner Nationalist not have wanted to destroy? The country that he wanted to destroy—did he feel that he truly owned it?

Now he feels it is more his than ever before, and he is less eager to shed his blood in its name, and so much the more eager to live in it. So the emphasis has shifted from naked *baasskap* to the more famous word, *apartheid*. Piteously, the Afrikaner Nationalists plead that they, like any other national group on earth, are entitled to a country of their own, and that South Africa *is* their country—which is true, and yet not true, for unlike any other national group they have never had a country of their *own*. They have always shared South Africa with the Africans, who are now beginning to claim the country as their own too. So from the truth that if they are to live in it at

all, the country must be shared, the Afrikaner Nationalists re-
coil into the monstrous delusion of *apartheid*. Let the Africans,
they say, have a country, or countries, of their own, within
South Africa; as long as we can have a country of our own there
too. We will create 'Bantu National Homes', the Government
cries; we will divide South Africa justly and impartially and
live in our separate communities as equals.

As equals? No, not quite.

The Bantu National Homes are to be the already eroded,
overcrowded and hungry Reserves, slightly expanded. (Though
no expansion has yet taken place.) Cities, mines, fertile farmlands, are all to remain in 'white' South Africa. Within their
Bantu National Homes, the Africans are to have self-government, 'when they are ripe for it'. In the meantime, every single
official is to be appointed by the white South African Government, which alone is to decide when 'ripeness' has come to the
blacks.

So much for the putative Bantu National Homes. What about
'white' South Africa? Is that to be denuded of the black
labour on which its economy totally depends? By no means.
The blacks are going to continue living in the 'white' areas, but
on the understanding that they are 'visitors' there only, and
thus not entitled to any political rights whatsoever. True, they
will actually *be* residents; millions of them will be born in the
'white' areas, in the cities and on the farms, and will die in
them too; but in some mystic and unexplained way they will not
belong where they are born and die, but to their distant and
as yet non-existent 'National Homes'.

Such, in outline, are the main projected developments of the
apartheid policy. These outlines may be decorated as taste and
inclination suggest. For instance, when those Bantu National
Homes are fully established, each smashed tribe in its own
Home, the Homeland authorities are going to appoint 'ambassadors' to the 'white' areas of South Africa. These ambassadors
are not, however, to represent the Homeland in the courts of
the white government (that would be pointless, seeing that the
white government appoints the Homeland government, anyway). No, these ambassadors are going to represent to the
blacks who live in the 'white' cities their own—that is, the

blacks' own—Homeland. Can you work it out? This will have the effect, you see, of creating *loyalty* among the urbanized blacks to those Homelands of theirs; and a very important task it will be too, seeing that none of them will ever have seen their Homelands. And do you know what is the shape of the ideal city-of-the-future, according to Dr Verwoerd? The ideal city-of-the-future, according to Dr Verwoerd, is to be round, and cut into segments radiating from a centre, like a sliced cake, with a different race in each slice. (For there are not only blacks and whites in South Africa; there are Cape coloureds, Indians... any number of possible classifications.) Then, you see, each race will be able to travel to and from the centre of the town *without ever crossing into the territory of another race*! And this bizarre, multicoloured, and segmented city, it must not be forgotten, is to be situated in what is solemnly, as a final touch of absurdity, always called *white* South Africa!

Grotesque? Laughable? Paranoid? Certainly. And all the more dangerous for being so. I will give later my reasons for saying this: at the moment I want to repeat that all of what I have written above are the Government's hopes or plans for the future. In the meantime, and with an eye to this idyllic future, things are much simpler; all the Government has to do, as the first step in implementing its policies, is to make it plain to the blacks that they don't belong where they happen to be. And this has been most zealously done already. Politically, economically, socially, every miserable little right the Africans had—of representation, of consultation, of organization—has been taken away from them; the 'pass laws' have been made more stringent; and the policy of 'separate facilities' has been introduced even in places where it was unknown before. (And heaven knows there were few enough places in South Africa before where black and white could ever mingle casually.) In addition, penalties of the most severe kind have been introduced for any infringement of the Government's new laws: for example, if you urge a black man to stay away from work, and he does so, both he and you run the risk of being flogged, jailed for five years, and subsequently banished to a remote part of the country.

But this, all *this*, is not oppression, the Government assever-ates; they are merely the measures preliminary to carrying out the policy of 'positive *apartheid*', as described above. And now that the word *apartheid* has fallen into international disfavour, the Nationalists are trying to think up alternatives to it. *Aparte ontwikkeling* (separate development) is one phrase that has been suggested; another is *aparte vryheid* (separate freedom).

In a way, I suppose, the fact that the Afrikaner Nationalists feel the need to talk of *aparte vryheid*, rather than of plain *baasskap*, is an advance of a kind. But if it is an advance in one direction, it is a retreat in another. The talk of *baasskap* at least had a direct and evidential relationship to the facts of South African life. The talk of 'positive *apartheid*' or *aparte vryheid* has no relation at all to anything visible, or anything conceivable, in modern South Africa. And I repeat that it is the total unreality, the dreamlike and fantastic character of the Government's utterances that makes them most dangerous. It is this, too, which helps to give the events in South Africa their distinctively twentieth-century character.

Of course, the South African problem is usually seen as being very much a part of a particular series of twentieth-century events: the throwing-off, by the former colonial peoples, of their white overlords. And it is true enough that these events are a factor of incalculable importance in the development of national consciousness among the blacks in South Africa, and one that is likely to become more and more important to them, as the territories to the north one by one assume self-government. But the comparison of South Africa with the other territories of Africa, and with the new states of Asia, is not altogether acceptable. There is one great difference between South Africa and the countries with which it is compared, and that is that in South Africa the whites are not just officials, traders, and missionaries, as they were in most of the other colonial territories. Nor are they even white 'settlers', like the *colons* of Algeria, who insisted that they are before all else Frenchmen, and then only, if at all, Algerians. The white South Africans are true inhabitants of their country; most of them have never known any other, and the Afrikaners have not even the most tenuous links with any metropolitan power.

Once it is accepted that the whites in South Africa are there by right, as much *of* South Africa as the Africans themselves, the country's problems seem then to resemble not so much the classic colonial situation as a kind of paradigm of the history of much of Europe in the nineteenth century. South Africa is going through an Industrial Revolution very much like that which England underwent in the nineteenth century; the mass of its people are fighting for the rights of political representation which the people of Europe fought for a hundred years ago. And like those people then, the Africans are confronted with an oligarchy of wealth and power which seems determined, at almost any cost, to cling to all of its wealth and power.

But one cannot wage a nineteenth-century struggle in the middle of the twentieth century: every century uses its own weapons. And the weapons in the hands of the present Government in South Africa are indeed those of the twentieth century. They include Sten guns, Saracen armoured cars, walkie-talkie radios and jet planes (and would the Bastille have been stormed if its defenders have been equipped with these weapons? Could the people of Hungary, better-armed and a hundred times more skilled in modern combat than the Africans, prevail against the armed superiority of the Russians?) But the greatest weapon in the hands of the South African Government is the Big Lie, the delusion which is so far removed from reality that it cannot even be rationally controverted. The Nationalist Big Lie is, of course, the policy of *apartheid.*

Students of totalitarianism, like Hannah Arendt or George Orwell, have told us that in order to make effective use of the great delusion, one needs a press, a radio, mass rallies, youth movements, secret hierarchies of power within the Party itself; and all these the Afrikaner Nationalist movement has. One needs to iterate and reiterate the grossest untruths so often that even one's opponents, let alone one's supporters, find it impossible to believe the evidence of their own eyes. Above all, by acting as if the lie were true, one has to destroy in one's supporters their sense of where their material interests lie, so that for the sake of 'higher' ideological interests—that is, for the sake of the delusion itself—they will sacrifice their goods and their lives.

Compared with the Nazis of Germany, or the Stalinists of
Russia, the Afrikaner Nationalists are mere beginners, bunglers,
lazybones, lovers of the easy life; some of them even do have a
positive respect for the processes of the law and the traditions
of parliamentary debate.[1] Their supporters have not been
driven to desperation by hunger or any recent war; the leaders
themselves have a deep hankering for the good opinion of the
world. But they *are* trying to impose a delusion upon the real
world; and there are people among them who have announced,
repeatedly, that they would sooner kill and be killed than give
up one single fragment of their dream.

And one of the most dangerous things about the politics of
delusion is that its example must be contagious, by its very
nature. Already from African leaders one is beginning to hear
statements which in their unreality match those of the Government. 'Africa for the Africans!'—is that really a rational call in
South Africa, where black and white, Indian and coloured,
already live and must continue to live? Or to give another
example—'What,' I once asked a liberal white, who was
prophesying the imminent and total success of the Revolution,
'are you going to *do* with the Afrikaners, after the Revolution?'
The question seemed to irritate him; eventually he replied,
'Teach them to speak Zulu!' Thus, as brusquely as Dr Verwoerd
ever dreams of doing, was a nation disposed of.

Even with the best will in the world, South Africa's problems
would be extremely difficult to solve: indeed, I do not believe
that they ever can be 'solved' in any simple sense of the word.
Furthermore, one of the reasons why the country's problems are
so intractable is that there is so much justice in the claims of all
the contending parties. It is particularly necessary to say this
about the Afrikaners—and not only because I have written

[1] In the years before and during the Second World War the Nationalist movement in South Africa was directly infected by Nazism; and Dr Verwoerd himself
was found, in a court judgment given during the war, to have consciously used the
newspaper he was then editing as an instrument of Nazi propaganda. (Dr Verwoerd's explanation of the court's finding was that the judge was a Jew.)

In fairness, it must be added that successive Nationalist Governments, including Dr Verwoerd's, have tried to be scrupulously correct in their attitude towards the South African Jewish community. Unfortunately, the strain of the effort
has been all too visible, at times.

about them unflatteringly here. The Afrikaners are not in-
human monsters, altogether unlike any other people who have
ever been seen. For the most part, they are very much like other
people: most of them are conformists, who are taken along by
their society, as people are everywhere. And when one thinks of
them as a group, it is impossible to regard their past struggles
and their bleak future, without being moved by a sense of
profound compassion for them. They have never had a
chance, one cannot but feel: history has again and again
tricked and cheated them. Now they are trapped in their
own history; and they can escape from it only by making an
effort that almost no other people has ever been asked to
make.

There are real, as well as unreal, problems in South Africa;
there is a reason for, and reason in, the fears of the Afrikaners;
there is justice in some of the demands they make upon the
world. But to say all this is not to yield one inch in one's belief
that their present leadership has set itself on a course which
has made a complex and difficult problem a thousandfold more
difficult; which is turning the inevitable dangers of political and
social life in South Africa into the certainties of suicide and
murder.

I have never shared the views of those who foresaw in South
Africa a single violent and apocalyptic Day of Reckoning
approaching. To my mind, the Africans were, and still are, too
weak for any single paroxysm of theirs to overthrow the power
of the State. People outside South Africa do not appreciate the
sheer *size* of the white establishment in South Africa; nor how
irresistible is the might of a modern army and police force,
equipped with all the arms it needs; people do not know that
the white oligarchy in South Africa mans its own armed forces
entirely, so that there is no possibility of subversion from within.
Conversely, people abroad do not realize how much divided
among themselves the Africans are, how unskilled politically
and technically; how uneager they are t risk the little they have
for a cause which has only just begun to seem plausible to them.
For all these reasons it seemed inevitable that, rather than a
revolution, South Africa would have to pass through a series of

crises, very similar to the one it has just gone through, and the one which it had experienced previously in 1953.

That, I believe, is still true; but while it once seemed possible that the crises, and the pauses in between, could be prolonged indefinitely, for generations perhaps, this no longer seems at all likely to me. Ahead of South Africa there still lies a series of hideous days, scattered perhaps over many years; no one can guess how many. But not over generations. Not, perhaps, over a single generation. And this is true for many reasons.

First of all, the strength of the African attack in the recent crisis surprised everyone, including (I am told) the African leaders themselves. It is true that the outbreaks were beaten down, and the country now is silent again. But when will the next campaign take place, and what form will it take? It is impossible to answer these questions; but one cannot refrain from asking them. To compare the campaign of 1953 with the campaign of 1960 is to realize just how far and how fiercely the African people have come forward in the last seven years.

Then, the reaction of the world to events in South Africa is of the greatest importance, and, for reasons both of morality and expediency, it is going to continue to be strong and uniformly hostile. South Africa depends on the countries outside it for trade, for investment, even for arms; and even apart from any question of sanction or boycott, the condemnation of world opinion has an accumulatively weakening effect upon the morale of the Afrikaner Nationalist—precisely because of his particular historical sensitivity to insult. It is true that being sensitive in this way, insults and reproaches from abroad *may* make South Africa's leaders more fanatic in their paranoia than they already are. From my own observation, however, I would guess that even if this were true of the leaders, it would not be true of the followers; the hostility of the world unquestionably weakens them more than it strengthens them. They simply cannot stand being hated and despised, indefinitely, again and yet again.

And in talking of the morale of the Afrikaner Nationalist I have already come to the third reason why I believe the whites in South Africa might not hold out as long as their own physical strength would enable them to. The last thing I would want to

do is to minimize the gravity of the crisis the country has just
endured; yet I must say that the pressure brought to bear upon
the Government by the African campaigners was not, as things
go in this world, very great; it was never sufficiently sustained
over sufficiently wide an area really to threaten the authority of
the State. But to meet even this degree of pressure the Government called out the army, declared a state of emergency,
arrested hundreds of political prisoners, turned the country
upside down almost more effectively than the campaigners had
done. What more can they do next time, then? And next time
the pressures may be more severe, let it be remembered; and
may take forms which the Government has not yet even re-
motely been required to face. (Remember Ireland, Palestine,
Cyprus, Algeria?)

An army could deal with the pressures, whatever forms they
may take. But the white people of South Africa could not—not
over many years, not over generations. They are not an army;
they are people, with families, children, businesses, private
ambitions. It may be argued that so too were the *colons* of
Algeria, who yet managed to hold out for years against pressures
more severe than any that are likely in the near future to be
brought against the white South Africans. But the *colons* insisted that they were Frenchmen, and had the might of France
to prove their claim, an army of half a million to fight for them.
The white South Africans are quite alone; no metropolitan
power will ever come to their assistance; they will have to do
their own fighting, and pay for it all, out of their own purses
and with their own lives. I do not believe that even if they were
united among themselves they could do it for long. And they
aren't united; to the English the Government is an alien and
incompetent one; not all Afrikaners, by any means, are
Nationalists; the Nationalists, for the very first time, are beginning to show some tiny signs of dissension among themselves.

But the last and most difficult question of all remains: is it
possible to envision in South Africa a multi-racial society,
each group in it meeting the others on equal terms?

There are two sides from which one must attempt to answer
this question: the white and the black. About the blacks it is

often said that even if the whites in South Africa were now, in good grace and with the best of intentions, to begin making real concessions to the Africans, the latter are so enraged and embittered at what they have suffered that they will continue to work reasonlessly for a 'black South Africa'. And to support this argument people point to the case of the Rhodesias, say, where the blacks have been granted concessions that the Government in South Africa has not yet dreamed of, and where they nevertheless appear to remain implacable in their opposition to the whites.

The case of South Africa is, I believe, very different. After all, it is possible to imagine Northern Rhodesia clean of whites—for though it is a 'settler-colony', its white population can be counted in tens of thousands. But to imagine South Africa clean of its millions of whites, one has to be insane. And the blacks in South Africa are not—yet—insane. To this day they are grateful for friendship which is offered to them (though a riot-maddened mob is another matter); they are eager to learn the skills which the whites can impart to them; they are eager to benefit from the products of the white investment in the country. There is no doubt that the longer the whites maintain a brute-force supremacy, the more certainly will it be replaced, ultimately, and at unthinkable cost, by a brute-force black supremacy. But if the whites yield, crack, give way before too much blood has been shed, then the blacks will, I feel, be ready to live with them.

But even if that were true, is it possible to imagine the whites of South Africa ever admitting the blacks as their equals? To the overwhelming majority of whites in South Africa the blacks are at best objects of patronage; and at worst objects of loathing, dread, and contempt. Can these people change the attitudes which are bred into them by every shred of tradition, custom, and usage they possess? I have implied that habits of subservience among the Africans die hard; how much harder will be the death of the habits of authority and superiority on the part of the whites?

Well, I have never thought these habits will die easily; they will never die altogether, for no habit ever does, in history. But the same habits can assume very different forms and issue in very different actions when circumstances compel them to. And vague and unsatisfactory though this formulation may seem, it will have to do to describe the changes that may take place among the whites who want to continue living in South Africa; and these changes, once they begin, may take place much faster than now seems possible.

In talking of this aspect of the South African problem people often compare the country with the southern states of the United States. Look, they say, at the whites there, who cling to their contempt and hatred of the negroes, even though the negroes are so outnumbered, and offer no real threat to the dominance of the whites in the country at large. What can you expect, they ask, if such is the tenacity of human prejudice, of the whites in South Africa, who *are* outnumbered and to whose dominance a real threat is offered?

However, what is overlooked in this argument is that it is possible to reverse its terms and arrive at quite a different conclusion. Surely, it is *because* the negroes in the South are so outnumbered and powerless that the whites there have been able to afford their prejudices. What does it cost the Southern white to 'keep the Nigra in his place'? The economy of his region is possibly developed more slowly as a result; and his country as a whole suffers in its bid for friendship among the coloured nations of the world. But these are remote and impalpable considerations for the white Southerner, compared to the satisfaction of his immediate fears and aggressions. His livelihood, whatever it may be, is placed in no danger when he puts on his robe and prances through the streets of a Southern town; still less is his life.

But in South Africa, 'keeping the Kaffir in his place' may well cost the white his livelihood and his life. And to keep his life and livelihood a man may well put aside others of his most cherished possessions: sometimes even his dreams, delusions and prejudices.

In any case, it must not for a moment be imagined that white and black are not already living together in South Africa. It is true that every South African city is two cities; every town, two towns; every *dorp*, two *dorps*: one black, one white. It is true that every post office, public lavatory, railway station (even every footbridge over every railway station) is double; true that the white man goes into his cinemas and beaches and cafés and never sees any blacks, except for those who are working there; true, too, that these divisions are being extended with a frantic and sickening zeal, wherever one turns. Yet, in the face of whatever denials and divisions the Government may attempt to foster, anyone still in his senses can see that every day, everywhere in South Africa, without cessation, black and white men are meeting one another, talking to one another, learning from one another, becoming more and more like each other. This is the single overwhelming truth about the country, and it is a truth that continues whether or not there are riots, midnight arrests, liquor raids, pass raids, old oppressions or new *apartheid* legislation before the House of Assembly. Every unnoticed and unreported day that passes in South Africa ties the black and the white communities more closely together; and though the contiguousness arouses the hatred, it lulls too, it makes brothers of those who hate each other. And their brotherhood is figured forth in one fact which is hardly ever mentioned or commented upon: the fact that the 'whites' of South Africa are no longer white. If you come from abroad, from Europe, where you have lived for years among those who are truly European, it is impossible not to be struck by the admixture of non-white blood which has passed into the veins of those who claim still, after three hundred years, to be 'European'. In noticing this, we should not try to console ourselves with pictures of an ultimate indiscriminate peace which will come to rest over the country. Before then the generations must live, the present generation at least. And there seems no way for it to live other than badly, bitterly, wastefully, in pain. But if it is impossible to set a date to the bitterness and sadness, the waste and pain, it is impossible, also, to set a date to the life.

And that is why, whatever way the country goes, it will not, in the end, go the way the Afrikaner Nationalists want it to go. People hear much of the crises in South Africa; they do not hear of the indifference there is in South Africa, the lethargy, the greed. But as surely as the forces of enlightenment, compassion and justice, these human failings or weaknesses, too, are working against the Government. And this should cause us no surprise. To deny full humanity to others is to make the attempt to deny it—in all its strengths and weaknesses—to oneself. Proudly, boastfully, the attempt is being made in South Africa, as it has been made a thousand times before in a thousand different places; miserably, squalidly, painfully, it is going to fail, as it has always failed before.

1960

D

RIOT IN KIMBERLEY

THE TWO WEEKENDS BEFORE the Saturday of the riots had been troubled ones. Stones had been thrown at the police who patrol the African locations, stones had been thrown at the location buses, notices had gone up outside the municipal beer halls in the locations calling on all Africans to boycott the beer halls.

Yet for all this, no one was expecting serious trouble. Stones are often thrown at the police by Africans, and the municipal ban on the home-brewing of beer had been a long-standing grievance among the inhabitants of Kimberley's locations. True, there had been a new element in the preliminary troubles. The stone-throwers had shouted '*Afrika!*' when they had attacked the white man's police and the white man's buses—and '*Afrika!*' was part of the simple, effective slogan of the passive resistance campaign organized by the African and Indian Congresses in their struggle against *apartheid* regulations. In that campaign six thousand Africans and Indians had gone peacefully to jail in practically every town of importance in South Africa, including Kimberley. But if a drunkard shouts a political slogan, it is his drunkenness that is noted; if an African shouts a political slogan, habit is quick to remind the white man that he is only a Kaffir.

The first we heard of the riot in No 2 location, on that Saturday afternoon, were the ambulance sirens down Main Road, and the alarm bells of the fire-brigade. It had been a peaceful afternoon, previously, in our part of the town, with the summer sun shining on all the gardens kept trim by so many African servants. Then from our neighbours we heard the news that the police had opened fire again and again on crowds of rioting Africans. As the warm evening drew on, and the sunlight failed, the air of the town which even now I can think of only as a place of peace and heat on the edge of the desert to the south and west, was still wild with the sound of sirens. My sister ran into the house to tell us how lorry-loads of police had just been seen going down Central Road towards Green Point Location; the police had been armed with rifles and Sten guns, and as they had passed my sister they had waved, smiled and given her the thumbs-up sign, like soldiers anywhere in the world, calling to their own people, sure of their welcome, sure that the young girl will smile and wave back to them.

We had some sort of supper. Then it was night. The darkness was turbulent with noise. We knew that the serious rioting was in No 2 location, which is right at the other end of town; but why then was there so much noise in our part of town? We heard shots, and distant yells, and all the time the wailing of the sirens. We went into the street, and there the noise was louder, and seemed to be coming from all sides. Our neighbours too were in the street, standing at the gates of their gardens in little white-faced groups, talking quietly to one another. I went back into the house and tried to phone the offices of the local newspaper; the number was engaged, interminably, but eventually I managed to get through.

'What's going on?' I asked.

'I don't know,' the voice at the other end said. 'There's a bit of a do with the Wogs.'

'What sort of a do?'

The man was as cheerful as anyone could be. He positively chirped the news over to me. 'They've burned down the beer hall and the municipal offices, and a whole lot else. Churches, all kinds of things. We don't know yet for certain.' Then he said, 'They say that the latest score's eighteen.'

'What score? Score of what?'

'Dead Kaffirs.' I could see his grin. 'The police are shooting them like hell.'

'It sounds like it.'

'It's a bit of excitement all right,' the other replied warmly. 'They're teaching them this time.'

I went back and told the others what the man in the newspaper office had said. Then, while we were talking, we heard two rapid bursts of fire from a Sten gun, far nearer than any had sounded before. We had been hearing shots all the late afternoon and evening, but from a distance: these, however, seemed to be rapping at the darkness near by, as if at the end of the block, around the corner. We went into the street again, and for the first time I felt a direct, immediate fear for my own physical safety. There is a police station at the bottom of the road, about half a mile from our house. It was too dark to make out anything clearly; but we could see a blaze of lights around the station. And immediately I was convinced that the Africans were storming the police station; that soon they would be coming up Central Road, coming for us. There were a few more volleys of shots, each as urgent and yet as precise in sound as the last. Then we heard someone screaming, one voice screaming over and over again, before it was lost in a confused shouting of many voices. '*Mayibuye! Mayibuye!*' the voices were shouting. That word was said clearly, above all the other cries and shots, and the long wail of the ambulance dying away to a mutter.

It was a word we knew. '*Mayibuye!*' is the other half of the slogan in the campaign of defiance of unjust laws. Together the words '*Mayibuye Afrika!*' mean 'Come back Africa!' Come back Africa to the people to whom the continent belongs; the black people who have worked for us and have been thrown into jail by us, and whom we do not allow to enter our schools and theatres, our playgrounds and buses. Come back Africa to your people. We who have white skins have lost you.

We knew that we were lost, as the sound of the fighting died down, and our sharp physical fear of death by violence left us as suddenly as it had come; as we stood with our neighbours and heard them say that the police must shoot them down, that the Government should give every white man a revolver. And most decisively of all, we knew that we were lost when we wandered into the back yard of the house, and saw our two servants standing there. Ben and Betty have been with us for years, and we thought we knew them so well, and that they knew us, and there was friendship between us. But that night Betty stood in the door of her room, in the darkness, and Ben

stood leaning over the wall of the back *stoep* on the other side
of the yard, and we walked between them, past them, knowing
that they were looking at us, waiting for them to greet us, to
say a word to us. But they did not move or speak. For our part,
shame would not let us speak first; we could not bring out a
sound to the two dark people who stood unmoving in the
shadow of our home. They let us pass in silence to the door of
the house, and we opened it and closed it behind us, escaping
from that rigid, accusing silence.

And that was how the riot, one savage, hopeless rising against
the authority of the white race, touched me. Now that peace
and heat have returned to Kimberley, and Betty sings in the
kitchen as she prepares the meals, the event seems no more than
a dream, gone with the daylight. And most dreamlike of all,
and yet most revealing about our waking way of life, was the
immediate and overpowering fear of death at the hands of the
black mob. For the white police are stronger than any mob, and
can easily confine a riot to the African locations, leaving our
wide, white areas quite safe. Even those shouts and shots near
to hand were not, as we had feared, a mob storming the police
station, but only the police bringing their prisoners to Beacons-
field police station, the jail and the other police stations being
full. We were as safe that night, within our areas, as we are on
any other night in this country. For the whites have the guns.
On the night of the riot, those guns killed or seriously wounded
over one hundred Africans.

1953

AFRICA, WHOSE AFRICA?

Some Recollections of a Festival

IN THE MIDDLE OF the arena there was a row of men facing a row of women. The men wore short skirts of fur around their loins, bands of fur around their foreheads, necklaces of pods hanging down their chests, and anklets of the same pods around their feet. Each carried a shield of hide in his right hand and a short hardwood *kierie* in his left. The women were dressed in heavy bead skirts of blue and red and black, and wore brightly coloured kerchiefs on their bosoms. Their backs were bare but for the knots of the kerchiefs. When they moved quick red glints of light shone from the naked skins of both the men and the women.

Up and down in front of the row of stamping men one woman passed with small steps, bringing her heel sharply down on the earth after the toe had poised itself. The step was small and rapidly repeated, while above, far more slowly, her dark brown body heaved from side to side, as if the small movements of her feet generated the slower movement of her torso, as she went along the line of men, to stop at last in front of the man she had chosen. She stopped, and the men ceased stamping, and in front of the man of her choice she treaded the dust of the arena, her body still, only her toes pressing and kneading into the ground; deliberately and delicately she insinuated herself before him. Until that too stopped, and she stood watchfully for a moment, before turning with a laugh and running heavily to her place in the line of women.

The dust the dancers lifted was heavy and did not rise above their knees, so that the drummers squatting to the side of the rows of men and women could hardly be seen. The sound of the drums seemed to rise insistently from the beaten, flat earth itself, in the centre of the village. All around the arena were small circular huts, built of poles and clay, with pointed roofs of thatch.

The man who had been chosen by the woman came out smiling and stepping high. When he and the men behind him brought their feet down, all the seeds in the pods around their ankles rattled and shivered with a dry, sighing sound that did not linger but was caught in the shiver of the next foot lifted. And to this, and to the sound of the drums there was added another sound: a heavy swishing noise, as dry as the shiver of the pods around the mens' ankles, but far heavier and longer, each one coming like a gust of wind and then receding. Then the next whirr that receded, and the next, with a heavy undeviating rhythm that no wind could have. The women were moving the cheeks of their buttocks, and as they moved the beads lifted and fell, until their sound rose even louder than that of the drums. The women's bodies worked in a strange plunging movement to keep going the lift and fall of their buttocks. They stood in one place, not stirring from it; their bodies undulated and straightened, plunged again.

Until with a leap and a prance of his legs the man fell in front of the woman that it was his turn to choose; he was on his haunches for only a moment, before twirling back elaborately to the rank of men, leaving the woman to come out like the other who had gone before her. Only, where the men had come out smiling and lifting their knees high, the woman hung back and smiled and turned to the others. But the drums beat on, and the men sang their phrase repeatedly, and the women clapped their hands, and the chosen woman had to go out between the ranks and begin her dance. And by custom the men and women did not dance in pairs, but each danced alone after he or she had been chosen.

In the end, it was the women who gave up. Their line wavered and broke, and the women stood in pairs and groups; the drums shuffled into silence. So the men broke their line too, casually, half-relieved. But two men complained that they wanted to go on dancing, and the others cleared the arena for them.

Now the two dancers stood at opposite ends of the arena, and waited for the drums to start again. And this time the drums were beaten with single harsh strokes; and the men did not have their shields and *kieries* drooping in their hands, but held the *kieries* head-high, and their shields above their heads. Together they had lifted their weapons, and together they brought their shields down, in a swift twist of their bodies, and beat the shields flat against the ground. 'Hah!' they gasped out from their chests as they bent to the ground. Then they leapt upright once more, and took a few steps towards one another, before crouching as before. 'Hah!' They seemed alternately to trail reluctantly towards one another when they bent low, and then to be jumping towards one another as if no time could be wasted. And then they would trail again, their bodies bowed to the ground, their shields flat before them.

Sweeping the arena, they came to one another. Their approach had been animal-like, with rushes followed by pauses, watchful hesitations. But now they were face to face. So they rose slowly, and the drum changed its beat, and they brought their knees to their chests in a swirling movement; their whole bodies turned in a spiral as each knee was lifted and then thrust down again with all the force of the body behind it. They danced around one another in this fierce exaggeration of a footstep, and sometimes when one would be making this step, the other would tread lightly away on the tips of his toes, kicking away from himself with the delicacy and swiftness of a buck. 'Hah! Hah! Hah!' they said now, with every step, and the sound was not a word, it came from their throats, their chests, without volition. And the climax of the dance came when the *kierie* was lifted and the shield was lowered, as if the blow would come now, while the sweat was thrown from them in arcs of glittering drops, and the drums clamoured distantly, and the women raised an ululation of terror that sounded like grief. The men danced closer and closer in the posture of striking, until they were so close that their shields clashed and the *kieries* were lifted still higher and hung above their heads. But this was a dance, not a fight, and at that moment they dropped their arms, they dropped the *kieries*, and pranced away from one another. One face had been set in a pout, the other square and open in a show of teeth that had not been a smile, but now both faces relaxed. The drum-beats rose in a final roar, and the men went off with little kicks in the dust, and leaps, and jerks of their arms.

There was a round of applause from all sides of the arena.

'I thought the women were sweet—waggling their bottoms like that,' a girl said. She was sitting between two men, one elderly, obviously her father, the other young, perhaps a suitor.

'Their muscle control is remarkable,' the father said, moving a little uneasily on his chair.

'Lack of control, I'd say,' the young man said.

All three smiled, without much amusement.

They were sitting in a brightly-dressed throng of whites, on one side of the arena; on the other side there was an even more brightly-dressed crowd of Africans. It was mid-winter, but all the men were in shirt-sleeves, the women in dresses open at the neck and the arms.

'Still, it's a jolly good show,' the girl said.

'The whole Festival is a jolly good show,' her young man reminded her.

'It is, it is,' the father agreed.

The girl turned her sunglasses from the one to the other. The sunglasses masked her face, only her bright red lipsticked mouth could be seen, and the tip of her straight nose, and the shadowed skin of her cheeks. Her voice was flat, colonial, almost nagging. She said: 'It's much better than I thought it would be.'

'Oh, yes,' her father said, uncomfortable on his wooden chair. The seating arrangements were as simple as possible, so that the village would look as much like a village in the bush as it possibly could. 'Everyone has done very well.'

Everyone had indeed done very well. Above the trees, among the pavilions, there rose a slender white shaft, the Tower of Light, the centre-point of the Festival, around which, in sunshine and shadow by day and in bright coloured lights by night,

D*

there were ranged the elaborate pavilions of all the governments of Africa, and those of private industries in the colony and the countries in Africa outside it. There were innumerable large open-air cafés, there was the Festival Hall where orchestras and opera and dramatic companies imported from England gave nightly performances, there was an expensive night-club where artists from the continent performed in an intimate cabaret, there was a fun fair behind the main exhibition site, where a star of lights, a big wheel, revolved unevenly behind all the other lights.

The pavilions and exhibitions were all light and airy, and built in a recognizable, unserious, sketchy festival style, in which thickly-painted sackcloth did for concrete and wooden beams for steel. The daring curves and angles of the pavilions leaped and jibbed in white, brown and blood-red against the unfaltering blueness of the winter sky overhead. Lawns of quickly-growing grass had been laid down between the trees, and flowerbeds were everywhere; there were innumerable vistas along which the eye could travel or be taken pleasantly by surprise by a sudden break in the view. And there was the African village, with its dancing arena, and Africans brought into town from the tribal reserves to paint their paintings and dance their dances while the visitors looked on. The Africans didn't seem to mind, and the dances were strange and exciting among the arches and parabolas, the pretensions and gaieties of the various government pavilions. Loudspeakers distributed music from poles all over the festival site; but sometimes, in the afternoons, even at the far end of the site, the air would be disturbed by the sound of the tribal drums, competing with the piped, popular songs of the day.

The biggest crowds gathered for the dances; but at no time was the African village empty. When the other pavilions, in the blank midday pauses, were deserted, their shade unused, the pictures of social welfare developments in Tanganyika un-stared at, the model of the diamond mines in Kimberley unilluminated by the button that it cost nothing to press, when young men stood idle in the Hall of Industry with no one to whom they could explain the workings of the bisected jet-engine, even then there were throngs of people in the African village.

The urbanized, dandified, sophisticated Africans in clothes like those of the whites seemed to be drawn to the village neither by shame nor by patronage, but rather by amusement: amused they walked through the village, amused they watched the dancers, amused they made comments to the tribal Africans who sat half-naked in the sun making clay pots or threading beadwork necklaces. But the whites—the well-dressed, sun-tanned, tall, colonial-born whites—walked through more solemnly with their cameras slung before them, and their comments, even of the most stupid among them, were tinged with a kind of respect for a people who, even in the artificial conditions of the Festival, were patently doing what they took for granted they should do, and who had a way of life that asserted itself with some conviction among the foreign archi-tecture—a conviction made all the more appealing by the fact that what they were doing was a doomed activity, as the presence of the urbanized, sophisticated and amused Africans of the town testified.

The Festival site was so cleanly, carefully, successfully modern that it was always rather disappointing to come out of it and find oneself staring down one or other of the broad avenues that led to the centre of the town in which the Festival was taking place, and which would be there long after the Festival had been dismantled. For the town was an unlovely modern straggle of a place, dominated at its centre by a few tinpot miniature sky-scrapers of six or seven or ten storeys apiece, surrounded by others much smaller. There was too much space around these buildings, too much sand, too much corrugated iron stuck into the sand, too much grass growing breast-high against walls.

The tall grass was everywhere, even among the factories at the bottom of the town, in the suburbs where the whites lived, among the pinched sub-economic locations where the blacks lived; the grass grew all round the town in the veld which could occasionally be seen, dry and yellow and unchanging, shadowed only by the low wild trees, at the end of the otherwise most suburban of roads. Because it was winter, the dry season, the grass was stick-like, and every night all round the town there were smudges of red and black where the veld was burning in fires that scented the air, day and night, with a smell that was faint and inescapable—the charred, distant smell of destruction.

The last dance of the day seemed to have been the most elaborately prepared; yet it also seemed to be quite without any centre of life. The dancers apparently did whatever took their fancy, and what took their fancy was usually dull.

There were some half-dozen dancers, and a drummer. The drummer was the only one among them who was not wearing a mask of some sort and a special regalia. The others all wore brown and yellow suits made out of a raffia-like material that covered their bodies completely. Two of them had feathers stuck on these suits, and long, trailing trains of feathers; another two represented male and female figures, the female-figure having enormous pointed breasts made of the same material, and the male-figure carrying rather high up, at the point where his navel probably was, a pole that was so long that it seemed to be more like a denuded flag-staff than anything else. The fifth figure simply wore the suit, his being a bald-looking white in colour. The masks were made of a dark wood, and fitted closely round the faces of the dancers. There was no relief from the darkness of the wood where the centre of expression, the eyes and the mouth, should have been; instead there were only crude black holes, burnt out with a hot poker. Of each dancer only his toes and the bottoms of his feet could be seen, for the suits narrowed down into a kind of leggings at the ankles.

The first four dancers capered about. The drummer pattered away at his little drum and sang sadly to himself in the yellow light of the sun, squatting in the warm, red dust; and the four dancers went from one side of the arena to the other, haphazardly, they met in the centre, equally haphazardly, once or twice they bumped into each other, but each simply went on his separate way again. They could hardly have been said to be dancing, it was difficult to say what they were doing. They jumped about, they rolled about, they covered themselves in dust, they stood upright and shook their heads, they waved their arms again. The drummer did not look up, he watched the drum between his legs and drummed lightly and sang to himself,

And this went on and on. Who could tell how well or badly they were dancing? Who could tell what they were trying to do?

Then the fifth dancer, the one in the bald white suit, began dancing, and it was easy to see what he was doing. He wasn't a dancer so much as a mimic, and for us he mimicked a monkey, a lizard, a bird that couldn't fly. He ran chattering across the ground, pretending to be a baboon, and squatted on his hind legs and made a grab at a pretended insect, and then examined the insect in his paws, as a baboon might. But the man didn't believe that he was a baboon, and didn't want us to believe that he was a baboon. He was never anything but a man trying on the role of a lizard, or a bird that couldn't fly. Trying it on, trying it on: there was something strangely cold about his performance, about the way he had no conviction and generated no excitement, and yet went on with it, over and over again, as if compelled to do so.

At last the drummer changed his beat, and the other dancers began clapping their hands, and they skipped around the arena and indicated to the members of the audience that they too should clap their hands. Very few among the whites clapped their hands, but the Africans obliged, and soon there was a slow, steady handclap echoing in the arena. The girl in the sunglasses, between the two men, was among the few white people who were clapping. One could see that she was demonstrating how young she was, how carefree, how enthusiastic; and she looked from man to man on either side of her to make sure that they too had seen. She too was trying it on, trying it on.

To the sound of the clapping the dancers suddenly left the arena, without warning, and though for some minutes the audience clapped on they did not re-appear. Then the loudspeakers crackled and a voice announced that that was the end of the afternoon's entertainment in the arena. A little dissatisfied, a little puzzled, a little dispirited the members of the audience got to their feet and began making their way irregularly out of the mock African village.

1955

A VISIT FROM ROYALTY

THE ROYAL VISIT WAS the most ballyhooed event that I can remember in South Africa. The royal family was dinned into us from every newspaper, every cinema, every wireless broadcast, every shop window, every decoration hung across every street. The royal family was here; the royal family was there; the royal family did this; the royal family did that. They had been in South Africa for weeks before they arrived in Johannesburg, and by that time hysteria was inescapable. A female announcer of the South African Broadcasting Corporation burst into tears over the air when the royal family came round her corner; a reporter on one of the dailies claimed that he had been stopped by 'an ordinary man in the street' in one of the Reef mining towns, who had exclaimed: 'What a golden eagle among men is the King!'

And at last, one rather cloudy day, the royal family came to beflagged, ecstatic Johannesburg. I saw them in the morning, rushing up Eloff Street in an open car, with outriders on motor cycles, and a ripple of applause coming from the people, fading before it had begun; the car was gone so quickly. The royal car was followed by a succession of big American cars with nameless people in them, all moving at a breathtaking pace. The police-men relaxed, an officer took his hand away from his cap, and the people turned to one another with reluctant, drawn faces, like sleepers awakened from a dream. People began picking up their folding chairs, children ran across the street where the cars had passed, the crowds on both sides of the street broke up, wavered, walked towards the station or the tram termini, carrying the little flags they had hardly had time to wave. I do

not know what the people had been expecting, for I had not
been among them before the convoy of cars had come past, and
had, indeed, been taken by surprise by the tired, known faces
rushing past, and the quick, too-late applause. The people
dispersed with no exaltation or disappointment: they were
strange to see at that moment, as though one were in a thousand
bedrooms as day returned and the sleepers reluctantly admitted
the light between their lids.

In the evening the emotions were different. With night, with
darkness, with the thousands of coloured lights, the crowds were
awake and wild. All over Johannesburg there were huge throngs
of people, walking, yelling; the bars were full and noisy; and, as
one does so often in Johannesburg, one caught the feel of
violence in the dark streets with their buildings towering on
either side. There were no Africans about; for their own safety,
perhaps, they had kept away. The liveliness of the streets that
are usually empty of pedestrians after nightfall had something
terrifying about it: the city was alive, bristling like an animal.
And the passion that filled the people, that drove them to walk
up and down the pavements, and in and out of bars, that made
them wait on street corners, and change their places repeatedly
on the stands, was elemental and powerful. It was curiosity.

I have never known anything like it. There was a huge animal
passion of curiosity among the people, that was like a hunger,
and was later to become a rage. They walked and waited and
talked, with an anticipation so intense one might have thought
something without which they could not live was about to be
shown to them. It seemed to be some final, lasting knowledge
that they were seeking; a spectacle which would satisfy them
forever. And all the night was tedious and tense, until that
moment would come. Then they, who lived so far from Europe,
from England, from Buckingham Palace, would at last *see*.

We waited. The policemen forbade people to cross Commissioner Street, so we settled down hopefully on the stands;
then became restive again. Someone threw orange peel at a
policeman, who fell into a rage, and drew his baton. He said
he'd kill the person who did it. But the crowd told him to shut
up. They called him Major, and Colonel, and, in an even
wilder flight of fancy, Field-Marshal Smuts. So the young

constable put his baton away, muttering to himself. Then a new sport began. People started slipping across the road, and the policemen tried to stop them. A man would wait until all the policemen on a particular stretch of road were busy chasing someone else, and then he would dash across, a small hurrying figure running across the dark tar, with the policemen after him. If he did manage to get across, a cheer went up from the crowd; if he didn't, a groan of commiseration. People called to the police, distracting their attention to help others. It was all quite good-humoured, but eventually one of the policemen hit one of the people he had caught with his baton, and the game ended in anger.

But we soon forgot the man the police had dragged away with blood coming from his forehead. We were waiting for the two princesses to go to a ball; and now young couples who had been invited to the ball were walking down the middle of Commissioner Street, the men wearing evening suits and the girls in long dresses. So we cheered them, mockingly and enviously; for white South Africans are democrats among themselves, and do not readily admit anyone else's right to be cheered just like that, unless he is a politician or a rugby player. The people we cheered were also white South Africans, and so were embarrassed by the cheers; when we saw that we cheered even more loudly, of course; and made rude remarks about the girls. '*Sis!*' a woman next to me exclaimed, in protest against the behaviour of the crowd, 'These people have got no respect.' She must have been one of nature's Englishwomen, for the rest of us had no respect at all, and no shame at not having any.

But all this, we knew, was preparatory, and everyone was relieved when the last of the couples had gone, the street was cleared, and the policemen came to attention. 'When they coming, General Smuts?' someone asked the policeman nearest to us. He said: 'Two minutes' time,' and we settled down in silence. We hunched, waiting for their coming. Then—a bright glow of car headlights, and a shout from the people farther down the road, the shout coming nearer, not yet really loud, and then it was upon us—a glimpse, a vision of pale glittering faces in a black car that was past us, again, before we could really shout, before we could really do anything. And now it was gone. There was nothing now, except for empty Commissioner Street, and the receding tail light of a motor-car and some motor cycles.

Nothing had been given us. As in the morning, there was a momentary silence, a kind of numbness. Then the animal awoke —not begrudgingly, as in the morning, but with a full throat. A roar went up from the crowd, a huge animal yell that rang in the streets. All along the road people were shouting, in a great, cheated roar. No answer had been given to them. And the yell died into silence as suddenly as it started.

A moment later the mob broke and began running down the road, past the Kensington tram terminus and towards the City Hall. People screamed and ran, from both sides of Commissioner Street. The police were unable to stop them. Jackets and dresses were flying loose, hundreds of feet were beating on the tar, hundreds of voices were screaming at the night, at nothing. A woman fell, and people jumped over her, or side-stepped to get away from what was just an obstruction in their path, and not a crying woman on the pavement. But no sooner had she been helped to her feet than she jerked away from her helpers and ran on screaming like all the others.

The princesses apparently had entered the City Hall through the door facing the Cenotaph, for our mob ran straight into another huge crowd gathered there. In the blaze of floodlights, people were pushing and screaming, and waving their hands though there was nothing to wave at, for the princesses had already gone inside. The crowd was possessed; in a rage, a frenzy, its passion unabated. Something had to be given to them —glimpses of two shining girls could not slake this thirst. So their passion focused itself on the nearest thing to hand: the car the princesses had arrived in. The car became their target— to see the car, to touch it, to hold it, to destroy it perhaps. But no, they did not want to destroy it. They just had to touch the car. They pushed and fought with one another, driving forward in surges. A woman next to me was carrying a baby in her arms, but she too was pushing, the child's face smothered in her sleeve. She screamed at me in Afrikaans, '*Eina!* You're pushing like a Kaffir!' and for a moment I remembered reading in one of the papers about the almost miraculous spirit of good will between the races that had been spread throughout the country by the royal visit. Miraculous, apparently, was the word. But that was lost, the woman, her words, the baby, as the crowd again gave a heave and we were all carried forward, this time right against the backs of the policemen who, with linked arms, were shoving us away from the car as determinedly as we were shoving towards it. The night was pandemonium; and all in a blaze of light that made every white face shine as though transfigured, that illuminated every open mouth and gleaming eye. And the police shoved the crowds back, shoved them back, until a passage was cleared and the car drove away, though a thousand voices called after it in a gasp, 'Ah!' and again, as the car turned a corner, 'Ah!' from the back of a thousand throats.

With some pushing I managed to make my way through the bodies and feet, hands and handbags, and finally get out of the pressure of the crowd, to the side of the City Hall. Few people seemed to be leaving: most of the crowd was still heaving about immediately around where the princesses' car had been. The last thing I remember before I left was a small, English-speaking South African, in a neat brown suit and shirtcuffs neat at his wrists, speaking to himself, or possibly to others, in the hope of whipping them into action that he himself was afraid to take. He was pointing at a group of Indian youths on the outskirts of the crowd, and his face bore that pale, fanatical look, self-absorbed, as though listening to God within himself, that white South Africans often wear when they are working up to violence on those with darker skins than their own. 'Look at them,' he was saying. 'Look at them. Filthy f—— coolies, coming to look at the King and Queen, as if they're white men. Look at them, f—— cheeky coolies. Let's do something.' His lips were trembling; the tremor spread to his hands. He stared at the Indians: he also was committing himself to a passion, perhaps one related to that of the crowds who, as the next morning's papers put it, had gathered to show their love for the princesses.

1953

Part Three

ISRAEL

ZION REVISITED

IT IS THE THINGS you don't remember, that you couldn't possibly remember, that come back with the most overwhelming sense of familiarity: you see them, you smell them, you taste them, and it is only your own wonder as to why you should notice them when they are so familiar and trivial—only this wonder that tells you how unfamiliar these scents, tastes and sights really are, how long a time has passed since you were last among them. Outside the Lydda terminal-building, the smell of Israel was at once in my nostrils, and though I had not known before that I knew the smell, I recognized immediately what it was. There was the sea in it, and sand, and orange blossom—but one can no more describe a smell than one can remember it, until one smells it again. And as with smells, so too with tastes, and the sight of such things as the illuminated black and yellow boxes advertising 'Nesher' beer, the white enamel plates with black lettering that doctors use to advertise their specialities, the look of a *gazoz* stall, the sand which drifts through the cracks in the pavements of Tel Aviv. These and a hundred other things which I had forgotten were the most sharply familiar of all; the things I thought I had remembered, I found most changed. The mind distorts what it consciously remembers, keeps intact what it imagines it has forgotten.

Ten years ago it was, in a way, easier for me to deal with my own experiences in Israel. I had come to Israel with half a mind to settle there, deliberately seeking an involvement with the country. But on the present visit, made ten years after the first, and very brief and unexpected in itself, I went there simply as a

tourist, leaving behind my career and my family in the country
in which I lived. I was merely going on holiday: after an
English winter I looked forward to being in the sun, to eating
oranges, to hearing a strange language in my ears and looking
at places which I could not expect soon to look at again.

I was in the sun, I did find myself in places which now seem
remote to me. But I was not like a tourist in any other country,
and I know that in Israel I never can be; it disturbed me to
find that I did immediately feel involved in the country, and
still do; and to have to admit too that on my return to the
country which I think of as 'mine' and the life which is certainly
'mine' I feel a deep discontent and impatience, even a resentment, that it should be as it is, and not otherwise. But how
other would I wish it? I do not know. Certainly when I was in
Israel I was often thankful that I was no more than a visitor to
the country, and that I would soon be going from it back to
England.

There are many good reasons why someone from England or
America can feel glad that he is not an Israeli. Israel is a
country that has been made out of pain and suffering; a country
where the parents, brothers, sisters and children of almost every
other person one meets have been killed by bullet, gas and
torture; and being there, one cannot but be oppressed by the
knowledge of what this had meant and still means to the people
in it. Then, Israel is a very poor country—how poor I had not
realized until the present visit. Its farmlands are tiny, its
industries are still largely artificial, its hopes of earning a
Western standard of living for itself remote. And much of Israel
is very ugly—not the country itself, which is harshly and
poignantly beautiful—but the towns and the villages which
have been built on it. One doesn't have to go far in England, it
is true, to find ugliness caked and irremovable upon the ground,
roofs like scabs, streets like jaws, acres upon acres, suburbs upon
suburbs of such ugliness. Yet there are great parts of London,
for example, which are beautiful to see, and even what is
immediately ugly in London can be transformed by its relation to the great patterns of the city. There is no city, no town,
no village in Israel about which this can be said, with the
exception perhaps of Jerusalem, perhaps of Haifa. Everywhere

else what one sees is shallow, disordered, scratched up, knocked
down, cheap, fragmentary; and this ugliness is curiously
exhausting and dispiriting, not only because there is so little
relief from it, but because one feels it to reflect again the
poverty and unhappiness from which it has arisen.

Now I know it will immediately be said: for heaven's sake,
what else could you expect? The country *is* poor, the people in
it *have* suffered, beauty cannot be catered for when the population of the country has tripled itself in ten years. All of which is
true; and nothing I have said affects my admiration for what
the Israelis have done in the last ten years, both in relation to
the enormity of the tasks thrust on them, and in relation to what
they were at the beginning of that time. And this is true of every
sphere of Israeli life: true of the houses they have managed to
build, of the people they have managed to train, of the roads
they have built, of the wastelands they have turned into fields,
fishponds and orchards, of the wars they have fought; true of
their attitudes towards one another and towards the State they
live in. The wonder is not merely that in spite of the population
having tripled within the last ten years living conditions are now
so much less harsh than they were; nor merely that in spite of
the unabated hostility of the Arab world there is much greater
confidence than ever before that Israel will survive, and survive
in strength; nor merely that as a result of the greater physical
comfort and greater security, the manners of the people have so
much improved, have become so much more relaxed and casual
that it is comparatively (though not absolutely) pleasurable to
drive in a car down Allenby Street—the wonder is something of
which these are all parts, and yet that is greater than any single
one of them. What most arouses one's wonder is the sense one
has of a constant, unending struggle in Israel to keep up
standards, and even more, *to find out* what the best standards for
the country really are. Without that none of the other achievements would have been attainable; nor would they promise as
much as they do for the future.

Fitfully, erratically, wrongheadedly often, but always determinedly the Israelis are trying to establish and live up to their
own standards; standards which would be meaningful and
distinctive within their country, with its problematical past and

future, its multiplicity of traditions and hopes. The fact that the
Israelis sometimes fail to find their standards, or fall into sheer
confusion, is unimportant compared with the fact that they try
for them; ten years ago one could do no more than hope that
this might happen, one could not really expect it.

For this achievement it can be said paradoxically that the
Arabs deserve something of the credit. The fact that Israel has
been under constant threat (indeed under constant attack)
since the inception of the State has—quite apart from the
physical suffering, the brutal, recurring loss of life that it has
caused—depleted the country economically to a degree that can
hardly be measured; that can merely be guessed at by seeing the
prominence everywhere in Israel of the army and its institutions. But on quite another level there is no doubt that the
sense of constant threat has strengthened the Israeli sense of
community, the sense of responsibility the Israelis feel towards
one another and to the country; they know they need one
another, and they know now that they can rely on one another.
And this feeling remains powerful and coherent in spite of the
fact that the problem of sheer survival is one that does not seem
much to trouble the Israelis any longer. Nor should one overlook
the role of the army as an educative influence in the life of the
country. The army has taken in thousands of young immigrants, and taught them not just how to be soldiers, but how to
be Israelis: taught them Hebrew, taught them trades, taught
them what it is to be answerable to the community for their
actions.

Discussing the role of the army in Israeli life is as good a
point as any to illustrate what I meant by saying that in Israel
the attempt to maintain standards is simultaneously a search
for what are or could be the most suitable standards. Before
returning to Israel, I had wondered about Israeli 'militarism',
which is something we hear a great deal about: the general idea
people have of Israel nowadays is that it is a kind of Sparta,
where even the girls carry guns. (Especially the girls carry guns,
according to the illustrated papers.) And I was prepared to dislike Israeli militarism as much as I dislike any other, when it
grows too big for its boots. In fact, and inevitably, as I now
think, I saw no signs of such a militarism: being in Israel one

soon realizes that there is little room for a traditional kind of militarism to grow. The Israelis are too democratic, too talkative, too untidy, too interfering, too independent, for the army or the officers' corps to take to itself powers to which it is not entitled, even if it wanted to—which it obviously does not. There is very little spit and polish in the Israeli army, there are no socially *élite* regiments (the idea is unthinkable in the context of Israeli life), those officers who are politically ambitious have to shed their uniforms and go meekly into private life before they are able to realize their ambitions. But if anything Junker-like or junta-like is unimaginable in Israeli terms, there remains the need for an *ethos* which can be transformed into a military quality should an emergency arise: if the Israelis don't admire the military mind and the military man, what do they admire? The answer is a curious one; and it typifies exactly what I mean by the Isreali need for their own standards of judgment and value. The 'military' qualities which the Israelis seem to have decided upon as most worth admiration are those of physical hardihood and physical daredevilry—precisely those qualities which the country's army most needs, and precisely those which are least dependent on the old kind of militarism.

Of this daredevilry the suicidal marches to Petra, in Jordan, are the most dramatic examples; but there are others, less dramatic, but not less significant overall. Anyone can join in the annual march to Jerusalem (this year some twelve-and-a-half thousand people were involved in it); any boy can try to join the paratroopers; anyone can go for a hike in the Negev along trails that only he knows about (the army was called out three times in the couple of weeks I was in Israel to find lost groups of hikers); and those who spoke admiringly of the Chief of Staff who had retired just before my arrival in the country referred first and immediately to his personal bravery, as though that were the quality above all others which most fitted him for his task. So, out of the need of the country, and their own deepest inclination of spirit, they have made a value, their own kind of value. And what is true here is true of other areas of Israeli life; true even of those where the issues are much less clear-cut, the needs more various, the inclinations more devious.

That there is a 'crisis of values' in Israel is a commonplace.

It can be described very crudely as a conflict between the collective pioneering values of the past; and the personal comfort-seeking values which dominate most other Western societies, and which are beginning to be dominant now in Israel too. To my mind, the 'crisis' is going to persist indefinitely; it seems to me a healthy and inevitable development that young Israelis should find themselves wanting to live private lives, and to pursue their own concerns rather than the concerns of the community or the State. But it also seems to me beyond question that the pioneering, democratic, and collective values of the early days will continue to exert a powerful influence on the thinking and feeling of most Israelis, and on their style of life. Again, the Israelis are being forced to find their own distinctive modes of valuation: the point is that the search goes on.

Jews have always been in the very centre of the cultural and social and religious history of Western civilization. And somehow people had imagined that though the Jews were 'normalizing' themselves in Palestine, they wouldn't normalize themselves to the degree where this knack or fate of theirs would disappear. On the contrary, Jewish and Gentile Zionists alike prophesied immense cultural, spiritual and religious contributions to be made to the world by a restored Jewish State. 'And out of Jerusalem will go forth the law'—surely, people believed, that would be true of a restored Jerusalem. And the kind of experiment in collective living made by the *kibbutzim* confirmed everyone in that belief—until now. Now the *kibbutzim* play a smaller role in the life of Israel than they ever did; and Israel plays a tinier role in the world's intellectual life than anyone could ever have expected. There they are, these Jews in Israel, trying to make a living in a very poor country, speaking a language that no one else on earth speaks or wants to speak, thousands of miles away from the Europe that gave the country its birth, isolated from the countries around them, populated by immense numbers of non-European Jews—whatever people expected Israel to be, it wasn't this. It wasn't a country where some writers write in English rather than in Hebrew, so that their work will reach the audience they want it to reach; where painters take their paintings to Paris and

London and New York to get the kind of appreciation and monetary reward they need; where students at the Hebrew University have to learn English in order to pursue their studies; where conditions, in many important respects, are those of cultural provincialism or colonialism.

Now some Israelis who care about these things react to this situation in the way of chauvinism: they deny that the problem exists at all, they make exaggerated claims for Israeli poetry, architecture, intellectual achievements generally. But these people do not deal with the problem: they merely exacerbate it. Fortunately there are others, many others, in Israel, who are honestly surprised and taken aback to find themselves living in what they recognize to be the provinces, and are wondering what can be done about it. Because they too had within themselves the conviction that Jewishness is centrality; now they are finding that Israeliness is not.

I had imagined that the decision of the overwhelming majority of the 'Anglo-Saxon' Jews to remain where they were must have come as a great moral shock to the Israelis—a moral shock not in any way diminished by the fact that the Israelis know how much they are dependent economically and politically on the continued existence of Jewish communities outside Israel. But I found that whatever the more ardent among the Israelis might have been saying a few years ago, they now neither expect nor even want the Jews of the English-speaking world to come to Israel. They are positively glad that these communities outside are there, for to the Israelis the Jews of the English-speaking world are one of their lifelines, their passageways, into the great world—the world which the Israelis, being Jews, are intensely reluctant to abandon. Israel is a small Middle Eastern country; but the Israelis want a stall in the world's great market-place of ideas, and they know that at present they are most likely to get one through their connection with the Jewries of the United States and England.

It is this which seems to be taking the edge off resentment: it is this too which offers to Jews outside Israel something more to do than raising funds. Fund-raising and fund-giving will have to be continued indefinitely, and for myself I cannot feel the contempt for the raisers and givers that has become fashionable among some members of the Jewish intelligentsia: the bread of too many people depends on it. But if money were all Israel wanted of the Jews who live in freedom and peace outside it, then the relationship would ultimately be a boring and enfeebling one on both sides. But Israel wants more, needs more: Israel wants immigrants, certainly, but she wants visitors too; Israel wants communication, dialogue, debate; Israel wants interest, concern, criticism; Israel wants to remain Jewish.

And what of the needs of the Jews outside Israel? No one can look ahead nowadays farther than a generation; for that period of time we can see that the Jews scattered over the world (outside Russia and its satellites) are going to continue as recognizable communities, however loose their organization may be. It seems unquestionable that these communities are better off in every way than they would have been had there not been two million Jews living in a country of their own; and if a catastrophe were to overwhelm Israel, a moral catastrophe would happen to them. (And very possibly it would be followed by a catastrophe of another kind.) And even if Israel were to survive as no more than a second-rate Levantine state, they would be the poorer for it, emotionally and morally. Whereas an Israel peaceful, reasonably prosperous and intellectually open is and will continue to be the cause of a particular kind of pride, a particular sense of release. There were people not so long ago who were making it their business to kill every Jew that they could lay their hands on; but they didn't destroy everything, they didn't kill everyone; and Israel, as it is today, even in its very failures, is a testimony to the will not merely to survival, but to survival on terms laid down by the victims, by those who were once helpless but are helpless no longer. If there was nothing but luck between any of us and Auschwitz, there is a bond of another kind between us and Tel Aviv. Historical bonds are easily forgotten; but this one is not historical: it lives. That is the bond.

I understand better now what it was that made me feel discontented and impatient on my return to England. What the Zionists have been promising us for so long is that once there was a Jewish State, the Jews within the State would become like any other people; the Jews outside would become, say, like the

Irish or the Greeks in America; all that was anomalous and without parallel in Jewish existence would be done away with. And in some way or another I must have believed that this had happened, or could happen, now that Israel had come into existence. But, being forced to consider the dependence of Israel on the Diaspora, and the involvement of the Diaspora with Israel, I realize that what the Zionists promised us hasn't happened, and isn't going to happen. There is no country in the world like Israel; and there are no people in the world who have a relation to any country like the relation which the Jews of the Diaspora have to Israel. What Israel has done, in fact, is to give another aspect of Jewish singularity—a new and very welcome aspect. But the singularity, the oddity, the anomaly of Jewishness remains what it has always been. (And by definition it remains that for the Jews of Israel too, no matter how much 'Jewishness' they are able to take for granted in their lives. Even the bare-armed and suntanned young men in the streets of Israel, with their confident, guttural voices, their cropped hair and fierce moustaches—they too had their secret place of bewilderment, their own puzzlement at what history had made of them; they too know and do not know what it is to be a Jew.) All the grammar books tell us that there are no degrees of uniqueness, that a thing is either unique or it is not; yet I cannot help feeling that the State of Israel has managed to make more emphatic, not less so, Jewish uniqueness.

Our uniqueness is in many ways such a burden, such a mystery, to those of us without religious belief who yet continue to be Jews. And to come to Israel, and to realize that not even in Israel, or about Israel, can the burden be laid down, is at first and inevitably dispiriting, disappointing. Was it for this that people toiled, and fought, and died of malaria, were hanged by the British, blown to bits by the Arabs—that we should still be different, and restless within our differentness?

Probably they did hope for more. Nevertheless, they have given us all it was in their power to give.

1959

THE GREAT MAN:

A Memoir of Jabotinsky

READING THE FIRST VOLUME of *Rebel and Statesman: The Jabotinsky Story* by Joseph Schechtman has reminded me that it is now almost twenty-five years since I met Vladimir Jabotinsky, when in 1938 he visited our home in Kimberley, during a South African tour. I was then a boy of about eight years old; and it has become as rather a shock to me to realize that I *can* remember something which happened well over twenty years ago. And much of it I can remember vividly, for it was my first meeting with anyone whom I knew to be without question a great man. My father had told me many times how great a man Jabotinsky was.

The programme—as I remember it—for Jabotinsky's stay in Kimberley was that he was to arrive on the morning plane from Johannesburg, that he would be met by a small reception committee at the airport, and then come to our house for lunch. In the evening he was to address a public meeting in the Town Hall; he was to leave the next day for Cape Town. Kimberley is a small town, and no doubt Jabotinsky did not attach any special importance to his stay there; indeed, for the children in our family the awareness of our own unimportance intensified our gratification at his visit. Nothing ever happened in Kimberley, we knew; yet it was to Kimberley that Jabotinsky was coming! And not merely to Kimberley, but to our own workaday commonplace house, which in its very familiarity was the obvious antithesis of anything which might have the name of greatness.

In expectation of Jabotinsky's arrival, the house itself became
less familiar. It was cleaned, swept, scrubbed; the lawns were
mown and watered and the flowerbeds were turned over; the
front *stoep* and the cement path that led to the garden-gate were
dyed with a special red substance which was brought to a high
polish by the African houseboy. In the kitchen a new dinner
service was unpacked out of straw and paper, and the back yard
was swept and raked. My father and mother discussed at length
the menu for lunch, and John the houseboy and Martha the
cook-girl were coached again and again in the serving of the
meal. We had had visitors before whom my parents had been
anxious to please, even some Zionist notabilities among them,
but never before had the preparations been quite so elaborate,
and never before had my father been as meticulous about
them as he was for this visit. To me all this seemed not in the
least surprising, for, as I can remember telling Martha, 'The
man who is coming here has talked to *kings*.'

What kings, if any, Jabotinsky had talked to I do not know:
perhaps I will learn from the second volume of Mr Schechtman's
biography. At the time I did not bother to ask. It was enough
for me to know that a man who had talked to kings was to talk
to me and my brothers, and to my parents, and even perhaps to
Martha. Our house shone for the visit; I wished that dusty, drab
Kimberley would do the same. But I knew it never would. The
burden of meeting the luminary with light was all our own.

In fact, the burden of greeting Jabotinsky was all my father's.
So far as the New Zionist Organization—as Jabotinsky's movement was known—had a branch in Kimberley, it was my father.
There were a few other 'New Zionists' or 'Revisionists' in the
town, but their adherence to the movement was lukewarm,
whereas my father's was passionate. I suppose the differences
between the 'New' and the 'Old' Zionists are pretty much
forgotten by now, even among Zionists; but twenty-odd years
ago these differences were, in our home at least, matters of
passion, of my father's passion. The Old Zionists, we were
brought up to believe, were pitiable, narrow, cowardly; the
New Zionists alone had courage and vision and understanding.
The New Zionists boldly demanded not the vagueness of a
'Jewish National Home' in Palestine, but nothing less than a

Jewish State in an undivided country. They insisted that if the British mandatory power would not accede to this demand, then Britain had to be fought, physically if necessary, inside and outside Palestine. And if the Arabs rose in opposition to the Jews, then it was the duty of the Jews to abandon their defensive policy of *havlagah*, and lay claim to the country by the strength of their arms—not by the piety of their methods of settlement. The New Zionists campaigned too for a mass exodus of the Jewish communities in Europe, whom they declared to be threatened by imminent death. And of all this, and for all this, Jabotinsky was the instigator and spokesman.

I shall return later to these aims and claims, and will try to describe a tiny fragment of what they helped to lead to, twenty years later, with a world war, a European holocaust, a campaign of terrorism, and two brief Palestinian wars between. At the moment I merely want to say that as a result of being a follower of Jabotinsky, and holding the views described above, my father had suffered something like a minor boycott in the small Jewish community of Kimberley. He had lost those communal positions he had held before he had announced his views; he had of course resigned from the local Zionist society; and there were certain leading figures in the community who would not greet him when they passed him in the street. Out of all this my father undeniably wrung a certain satisfaction; and it is just for this reason that I cannot help wondering what would have happened to his admiration for Jabotinsky if he had known him for longer.

In the event, Jabotinsky's visit was not an unqualified success from my father's point of view, though there was nothing that went wrong with it publicly. As I have said, the burden of organizing the visit was all his; and he carried it out efficiently enough. He was confident that Jabotinsky's name was sufficiently well known to warrant hiring the Town Hall, the biggest hall in Kimberley, and he did so; he saw to it that leaflets were printed and distributed, and that advertisements went into the local press; he arranged for the mayor of the town to greet Jabotinsky on his arrival; he inspected the room in the hotel where Jabotinsky was to stay overnight. And our own house, on the day, was all that he wanted it to be.

The whole family went out to the airport as part of the

reception committee. Apart from ourselves, there were three or four fellow Revisionists who had given some help to my father, the mayor, the local rabbi, and a reporter from the Kimberley daily. Jabotinsky was the first person I had ever met who had come in an aeroplane, but I hardly wondered at that; it seemed to me no more than fitting that he should come from the sky, in one of those planes which were then still rare enough to be stared at when they lumbered over the town. In a way, I was less impressed by the aeroplane than I was by the fact that the non-Jewish mayor of the town had felt himself called upon to join in the welcome to be given to our visitor.

Jabotinsky was small; he was dressed in a grey suit with a pale stripe; he seemed calm and self-assured, and more interested in us than I had expected him to be. But what struck me most of all about him was that he had some powder on his face. It was, I suppose, some kind of talcum powder which he had put on after shaving and which he had not bothered to wipe off; but it seemed then quite mysterious to me, and not a little embarrassing. What was even more embarrassing was that the mayor could not pronounce Jabotinsky's name. The reception took place in one of the waiting-rooms of the airport, to which my father had conducted Jabotinsky from the barrier, and the little room seemed crowded by the time the mayor began to speak. He spoke hesitantly, poorly, I thought, but he went beyond what I had thought could be Kimberley's worst when he called Jabotinsky 'Mr Jabber—— Jabber—— Jabbersky' every time he had to say the name.

I didn't know which way to look; I tried particularly to avoid meeting the eyes of my brothers who, like myself, were scrubbed, combed, and in their best suits. But eventually I looked at Jabotinsky. To my surprise, he seemed undismayed at what the mayor was calling him; he stood calmly and gravely, his head inclined a little, listening to what was being said. Then in reply he spoke a few words; I can't remember what they were, but I do remember feeling a little disappointed because he spoke with a 'foreign' accent, like any other Jew of his age. I believed that all Jews who were not of my generation spoke like 'foreigners', but I was expecting Jabotinsky to be remarkable in every respect. He was not in this one.

E

In what other respects he may have been remarkable, I can't tell from my single meeting with him, for my memories of what passed after the reception at the airport are vague and disordered. I think that after the strain of meeting the visitor I became bored and overwhelmed, and as a result was able to take in little of what was happening around me. I know that my elder brother was so overwhelmed that no sooner did we get home than he climbed on his bicycle and simply rode away. Lunch was delayed in expectation of his return; but we ate the meal with an empty place at the table. I can remember Jabotinsky inquiring just before he left the house about my brother, and my mother assuring Jabotinsky that she was not worried, and was sure her son would be back. He was, at dusk, exhausted after his ride, and ravenously hungry. Of the lunch the only vivid recollection I have is the expression on my father's face when John served up the dessert in the wrong bowls. Later in the afternoon my father took down the photograph of Jabotinsky which hung in our living-room, and removed it from its frame; Jabotinsky then inscribed the photograph in a beautifully neat hand. And for the rest I remember the unfamiliarity of the house, with its shining *stoep* and garden path, the servants glistening in their starched whites, the talk and the smoke and the bottles and glasses in the living-room, where the grown-ups gathered after the meal. I did not go to the meeting in the evening, and I did not see Jabotinsky again, after he had left the house. The meeting, I gathered the next day, had been extremely successful. Jabotinsky's name had been sufficient of a draw to more than fill the Town Hall with Jews and Gentiles, and my father was glad that he had charged an admission fee, to go to New Zionists funds, though others had advised him against it.

But Jabotinsky spent a longer time in Kimberley than he had planned to. Or rather, he spent the time near Kimberley. For after the meeting in the Town Hall he declared that he did not want to go to Cape Town the next day; he had no meeting to address there for a couple of days, and no appointments of any importance, and he thought that this would be a good opportunity for him to rest. My father, I understand, had offered him the use of our house, if he wished to leave the hotel; but

Jabotinsky had declined the offer. What he wanted, he said, was to be alone, quite alone, in a small place where there would be no one at all who knew him. He wanted, he said, 'to think', 'to ponder on certain matters'; he wanted 'two days of solitary reflection'. To me the request seemed all that might be expected of a great man; it had an imperious, poetic air about it which I much admired. But my father was disconcerted; he did not understand the request, and I don't think he altogether believed in its necessity. I could not then see the reasons for my father's disapproval, but I do now. I believe he suspected Jabotinsky, his hero, his one great man, of being a little moody, a little sulky or contrary; of being determined to show his differentness from everyone who did not need two days for 'solitary reflection'. And as a result of the change in schedule, my father had to do much telephoning and telegraphing to Cape Town and Johannesburg.

For his two days of solitary reflection, Jabotinsky went to a little village, Barkly West, which had once been famous as the scene of the country's first great diamond rush. Barkly West is about twenty miles from Kimberley. For a South African *dorp* it is an oddly cramped little place, though it has a fine view across the Vaal river, with the rocks in the river-bed shining in the sunlight and a trickle of dark green water running between them. Along the banks of the river, for a distance of many miles, the ground was turned over into heaps by the diamond diggers, during the late 1860's; some of these artificial hillocks are still bald, others are covered with a thin growth of grass and low camelthorn trees. But for miles upon miles of these abandoned mounds, there is hardly any sign of human effort or achievement around Barkly West; the veld stretches uncultivated to the horizon, on all sides.

There, for two days, Jabotinsky reflected.

Time destroys us all and forgets us all; but it never releases the living from the compulsion to act. Jabotinsky must already have been a very sick man during his visit to Kimberley; he had really needed that rest in Barkly West, though he had been unwilling to admit (perhaps even to himself) why he had needed it. Two years later he was dead; of a heart attack, in New York.

Last year I went with my father, who is now in his middle seventies, to Israel. One of the things we did while we were there was to pay a visit to the museum, run by an Israeli political party, which records the struggle of the Irgun Zvai Leumi against the British mandatory régime. A room in the museum is set aside for relics of Vladimir Jabotinsky, for it was to him, even after his death in 1940, that the Irgun looked for inspiration. In the Jabotinsky room there are manuscripts, many photographs (one of them an enlarged copy of the photograph which had hung in our living-room); in a glass case there is the uniform and ceremonial sword Jabotinsky had worn as an officer in the British army during World War I.

In the largest room there was the commemorative exhibition of the terrorist campaign, and memorials to the men who had taken part in it. There were photographs of the buildings the Irgun had blown up; models of the explosive devices which had been used; photographs of the young and middle-aged men who had lost their lives in the campaign, either in street fighting or by being hanged by the British. There was a knotted hangman's rope draped across one board; suspended from another was the collarless overall which the men had worn on the scaffold. Diffidently, proudly, or solemnly, the men in the photographs stared across these ghastly exhibits to others hardly less ghastly. To the photographs of a crowd of people with shocked faces staring at rubble and a corpse in the street; of illegal immigrants penned behind barbed wire on a tramp steamer; of a man being carried away by two of his fellows, his backside torn open by gunfire.

The worst that Jabotinsky had prophesied for Europe had come about; the wars he had anticipated in Palestine had been fought—and won. The State, for whose realization he had expended his life, was in existence. And the museum was deserted. The whole time we were there, only one other visitor wandered into it, a bored, lonely girl with a dissatisfied expression on her face; she looked as though she were passing the time while waiting for her date to arrive. And who could be anything but glad that the people outside avoided the place, with the smell of dust heavy within it and the horrors on display on its walls? The people outside had other things to do, other

interests to follow, their own lives to live. And there was no
irony in the reflection that that, just that, was Jabotinsky's
reward, the only certain vindication that anyone could offer on
his behalf.

As we came out of the museum, it was not just the glaring
sunlight and the hooting traffic which dazed and assailed me; it
was my own ignorance. I remembered the visit of the great man
of my childhood to Kimberley; I remembered my own incom-
prehension as to what the visit had been about. How much
more, how much better, did I comprehend now? I knew at
least what I had not know then: that time passes; that men
act; that out of their acts a history is made. But to what
purpose it was that we were hurled vertiginously through time
and history, I knew as little as I had known in Kimberley, when
I had stared in wonder and embarrassment at a small grey
bespectacled man with powder on his cheeks and a respectful
tilt of the head towards the strangers who had gathered to meet
him.

1960

Part Four

WRITERS AND WRITING

WHY READ NOVELS?

SOONER OR LATER ONE is asked the question, and sooner or later one has to muster up, for one's own sake, an answer to it. Of course the first answer is, 'Because I enjoy reading novels,' but that is insufficient, even for oneself. 'What is the use of it?' people want to know. 'Why should we bother?' Those of us who believe that the novel does provide more than a momentary enjoyment, and can teach us what no other art-form does, have to go on, we have to argue our case. And when we read some of our fattest and most authoritative critical quarterlies, we cannot help feeling at times that in order to argue the case we have first to rescue the novel from some of those who think of themselves as its warmest friends; from those critics who are so involved with it that they never ask themselves the outsider's honest query.

Ours is an age of specialization, as everybody knows; and everybody knows too that the only way to win respect from other specialists is by showing them that one's own speciality is just as special as theirs. But respect is something very different from attention, and it is attention first, and attention always, that the critic should be trying to gain for the work he is discussing. And it seems to me that one obvious way of doing so would be for the serious critic of fiction to make it plain that his specialization is not all that special and private, after all. Indeed, one of the first answers to the question, 'Why read novels?' is that in an age of specialization the novel remains singularly un-special; and, so far from this being anything for critics or novelists to be ashamed of, it is one of the glories of the form.

The novel really is knowledge: the recorded knowledge of

the states of consciousness of different men at different times. For most of us, for most of the time, one kind of knowledge or way of knowing excludes every other; we know abstractly or we know intuitively, we know sensuously or we know mentally. But the novelist, ideally, knows simultaneously what we know only in alternation; and within any single work he is able to deploy one kind of knowledge against another, to imply one when he is writing about another, to remind us of the others when we would prefer to read only about one. Continually, in his creation of character, the novelist is shifting, moving, comparing, remembering, uniting these kinds of knowledge. The characters in a novel are the novelist's individual foci of consciousness; they, ultimately, are what the novelist knows, and the greater the novelist the more characters he will be able to create and the more he will know about each one of them.

Already, here, we can see why the novel is so supremely important in this 'age of specialization', when we feel the multiplication of abstract 'knowledge' of all kinds to be not liberating but frightening and discouraging; when every publisher's crammed list and every learned journal is an invitation to us to give up the struggle for consciousness, with the feeling 'It's too much, it's beyond me.' The novelist can remind us again and again that what is important for us to know, outside our own specialities, is not too much, is not beyond us. The novelist cannot be expected to know about the latest developments in physics or medicine, say, but he can be expected to know what is to be affected by these developments; how they affect and alter our most intimate picture of ourselves. It is for this reason that the novelist can so much help to restore to us our sense of community—which nowadays is shattered not only by racial and ideological strife, but also seems to be broken anew by every advance that is made in the accumulation of knowledge about the physical world.

The help of the novelist is invaluable too in our consideration of the abstract programmes or ideologies which some people feel it is his duty simply to make enticing. The novelist must be capable of understanding the attractions of ideology, if only because so many men live by ideology; but, as a novelist, he knows that any political or moral abstraction has its real life and importance solely within the individual men who are affected by it. If for a moment the novelist should forget this then he is no longer imparting to us the knowledge which we ask from him. We say that he has become a propagandist; but there is another way of putting it, which seems to me more useful here—and that is to say that such a novelist has become as ignorant as the character he is creating; he has allowed his consciousness to become as shrunken and constricted as that of the ideologue. Consciousness again is the keyword: the novel is *about* consciousness, about the degrees, the modes, the states of consciousness which men have experienced. What the novel always strives for is a total consciousness, a total illumination of the experience which it attempts to describe. And as readers, we have to judge the novel by the extent to which it enlarges or falls short of our own total awareness of the fullness and variety of life as we have experienced it.

However, the novel does more than 'enlarge' our consciousness, more than show us how different and how similar we are to other people—vital and restorative though this work is, and especially so, as I have suggested, today. The novel also gives point and direction to our consciousness, in the very act of enlarging it. I can most clearly indicate what I mean here by giving an example; and I cannot do better than to take my example from Tolstoy, who, even to those of us who read him only in translation, must seem indisputably the greatest novelist who has ever lived. And the greatness of Tolstoy resides precisely in the truly astonishing range and depth of the knowledge he brings to bear (and forces us to bear) upon each of his characters.

When one begins reading Tolstoy one at first misses the particular personal timbre that agitates the pages of most other novelists; one wonders at his peculiar mildness and placidity of tone; one wonders how he seems able to say such very damaging things about his characters without seeming to hold anything against them. Take the opening scene of *War and Peace*, Mlle Scherer's famous *soirée*, and the description of Prince Vassili Kuragin within it—how he speaks from habit, like a wound-up clock, saying things he does not even wish to be believed; how he accedes to the request of Boris Drubetskoy's mother not because he wants to do her a favour but because he feels it would be more trouble not to accede; how he takes Mlle Scherer's hand at an important moment in their conversation 'and for some reason bends it downwards', as a way of imparting significance to what he is saying. In all this we see the man emerge, from the top of his 'perfumed, shining bald head' to his court stockings and slippers; but it is not the wonderful clarity and absurdity of the detail to which I want to draw attention, nor the economy and frankness of Tolstoy's means of displaying this detail, before our eyes, with no sleight-of-hand or fuss of any kind—it is the calmness of his tone. He doesn't seem to *mind* that Prince Kuragin is an old bounder, sponger, hypocrite, bully and liar; and at first his not seeming to mind is disturbing. Every other novelist we know *would* mind; we think how Dostoevsky might have writhed, Dickens might have jeered, Lawrence might have hated. Tolstoy simply lets the old man go on his way; and as Kuragin begins in the novel, so he continues, throughout, lying, bullying and sponging. (Though even he is given a moment of true dismay after the death of the old Prince Bezuchov.) He is a minor character in the book, and nothing very much happens to him, but by the end of the novel we know exactly what he is—and my point is that we know Kuragin not only through what has been written about him and what he has done, but also because we know what has been written about all the other characters. We know, because Tolstoy knew, all that Kuragin has missed, being what he is: how incapable he is of ever attaining the states of intense consciousness that are suffered or enjoyed by people like Andrey and Pierre, Natasha and Princess Marya. Kuragin, the creature of his society, is barely alive, barely conscious, deaf, deprived, inferior.

Plot is usually thought of as the great moral agent within a novel, what happens to a character being the judgment that is passed upon him. This is true enough, as far as it goes, but it does not go far enough; because in point of fact, as we have seen with Kuragin, nothing at all need happen to a character in any obvious overt sense, and yet he can be placed for us within a moral scheme. If we are to talk of reward and punishment, we have to say that the novelist does not (or should not) punish his characters; they punish themselves, being what they are: he does not reward his characters, they reward themselves, being what they are. The novelist *knows* them, better than they know themselves or we know ourselves; he knows them fully, he illumines them to our inward view. And there are as many ways of doing this as there are novelists and novels: *Moby Dick* is as different from *War and Peace* as either is from *The Portrait of a Lady*, but they are all great novels, great acts of consciousness.

I cannot help feeling that when people prophesy the death of the novel they are looking forward to the demise of more than a single art-form; they are half-hoping that the sort of power which belongs to the novelist will go out of existence. They no longer believe (or want to believe) that it is possible to try to know the human truth of every situation in which people find themselves; they resent the novelist's claim that we can be known, and shown, in our weakness and strength, by others, through all the changing forms of our changing societies. If it is true that the novel is dying, then so too is modern man's ambition to know the truth about himself. If the the novel lives it will be because that ambition lives still.

1959

F. SCOTT FITZGERALD

FOR MANY YEARS NOW Scott Fitzgerald's reputation has stood
consistently high; too high, one is inclined to feel at times,
considering on the one hand the kind of praise which is regularly evoked by his work from critics and reviewers; and
considering too, on the other hand, the very small quantity of
writing to which this praise can justly be applied. One cannot
help suspecting that some of the praise is still being given to
Fitzgerald by way of recompense, to make up to him for the
neglect from which he suffered in the later years of his life. In
any case, his high critical reputation has ensured that his life
and work are continually kept before us. Just in the last few years
there have been several reprints of works by Fitzgerald, the
most notable among them being the two volumes of *The Bodley
Head Fitzgerald*, which have brought together practically all the
writings for which Fitzgerald is chiefly remembered. We have
had too *Afternoon of an Author*, edited by Arthur Mizener, which
contains a group of hitherto uncollected articles and stories by
Fitzgerald; and it is not so long ago that Professor Mizener's
excellent biography, originally published under the title of *The
Far Side of Paradise*, was re-issued as *F. Scott Fitzgerald: a Bio-
graphical and Critical Study*. There has also been *Beloved Infidel* by
Sheila Graham and Gerold Frank, which is largely a remini-
scence of the years Miss Graham spent with Fitzgerald; and
this last book has been made into an atrocious film. When
Scott Fitzgerald died not a single one of his works was in print;
now his life and death are being hideously travestied in our
local picture palaces, with Gregory Peck in the leading role.

The disengagement of a writer's life from his work is always a delicate and difficult business, and in Fitzgerald's case the difficulty is notorious. His life was an extreme one, not least in the pain he endured; and we cannot absolve ourselves of our responsibility for it by saying that his pain was self-inflicted. Suffering of Fitzgerald's kind is always self-inflicted, and society is always responsible for it. Nevertheless, one must feel sufficiently free of guilt not only to respect, admire, and pity Fitzgerald, but also to confess to the irritation one feels with him. And one is irritated with him not because he spent his money unwisely, or did unforgivable things when he was drunk, or because he was drunk so often; but because he so often betrayed himself and his best insights; because he tried so hard to bluff himself about what he was doing. He never really succeeded in bluffing himself: if he had succeeded he would not have been either pitiable or admirable at all, though it is quite possible that then he would have been a happier man. Fitzgerald was never taken in; but how hard he tried to be, and how often the attempt mars his own best work!

Fitzgerald was a man with the most strenuous social appetites; and much of his work is a statement of the intellectual and moral cost of attempting to gratify these appetites. For reasons to do no doubt with his own psychological make-up, and to do certainly with the country and time in which he was born, the attempt on Fitzgerald's part to gratify his own social hungers was never unaccompanied by guilt and anxiety, was never less than exhausting; and in book after book, and essay after essay, he sought earnestly and hopelessly to imagine a way of life which would seem glamorous, graceful and free enough to warrant something of the energy he had himself expended in his pursuit of glamour, grace, and freedom. Only in one book did Fitzgerald face up to the possibility that for him and for his characters there was *no* way of life commensurate with his own ambitions and theirs; that the richness of his life and theirs was in the appetites themselves, and not in the objects of appetite. In his other work, driven as he was by a fear that his own struggles would be meaningless and futile unless he could, as it were, show something for them, Fitzgerald was again and again forced to try to pass off the inferior for what it wasn't; or else to gesture towards the genuinely superior, in spite of the fact that his art could not depict it.

We can clearly see him doing both in the very beginning of his last completed novel, the book on which he spent years of labour under extremely bitter conditions. *Tender is the Night* opens with an admirable description of the heat, colour and languor of a Riviera beach. Through the eyes of a young girl we are introduced to two groups on the beach: one group the girl finds very attractive, the other she dislikes. Eventually, she joins the group to which she is attracted, and listens to their conversation, which consists of some modish talk, a few catty remarks about others on the beach, and the description of a practical joke (the kidnapping of a waiter). Later we see another practical joke (one of the men appears wearing flesh-coloured bathing trunks), and then the party goes for a swim:

> 'Simultaneously the whole party moved towards the water, super-ready from the long forced inaction, passing from the heat to the cool with the *gourmandise* of a tingling curry eaten with chilled white wine. The Divers' day was spaced like the day of the older civilization to yield the utmost from the materials at hand, and to give all their transitions their full value. . . .'

A little later a warning note is struck:

> '(Rosemary's) naïveté responded wholeheartedly to the expensive simplicity of the Divers, unaware of its complexity and its lack of innocence, unaware that it was a selection of quality rather than quantity from the run of the world's bazaar; and that the simplicity of behaviour also, the nursery-like peace and goodwill, the emphasis on the simpler virtues, was part of a desperate bargain with the gods and had been attained through struggles she could not have guessed at.'

One's only reaction can be one of surprise and incredulity: whom is Fitzgerald trying to deceive? There is nothing that has been said or done by anyone on the beach which warrants a single one of the words the author is using about the group—and it is worth noting too that many of the words are themselves without any distinction at all. Still, even if one takes them at

the value the writer is trying to give to them, where is the
'*gourmandise*', the 'day of the older civilization', the 'simplicity',
'peace', and 'goodwill' in what has been shown to us? Yet this,
Fitzgerald assures us, is *it*, the real thing: 'At that moment the
Divers represented externally the exact furthermost evolution
of a class, so that most people seemed awkward beside them.'
One is embarrassed by his fervour, by his anxiety to talk himself
into believing what he is saying.

But really the author has given his own game away even
earlier. It was Fitzgerald's stated intention to have as the
background of the novel 'the leisure class . . . at their truly most
brilliant and glamorous'. How little faith he had in his own
ability to realize this brilliance and glamour is shown up
clearly by the fact that he chose to present the Divers to us—on
the beach which they had made fashionable, surrounded by
their closest friends, at high summer—through the eyes of
Rosemary Hoyt, who is seventeen years old and falls in love with
Dick Diver. Why should he take *her* word for anything? But
this is just what Fitzgerald wants us to do; he wants us to be as
dazzled by the Divers as Rosemary is. Of course he does at the
same time warn us that there is much about these people which
Rosemary cannot see; nevertheless, the author is trying here to
evade responsibilities which are his, and not Rosemary's; and
we feel the evasiveness of the tactic even more strongly when
we see how very little use is subsequently made of the girl.
One may as well add that this same sleight of hand was tried
again by Fitzgerald in *The Last Tycoon*, the much-praised,
unfinished novel he was working on at the time of his death.
There too we first see the hero, Stahr, the Diver-figure, through
the eyes of a college-girl who is in love with him, and again
we are clearly intended to take the college-girl's word for our
own evaluation of Stahr. Again, if we have any self-respect,
we do no such thing.

It must be emphasized again that *Tender is the Night* does not
rest at Rosemary's first impression of the Divers: it is supposed
to be an exploration of the 'complexity' of which the author has
warned us. But unless we believe in the Divers' initial grace,
brilliance and suppleness (even though they are 'external'), we
are unlikely to find Dick Diver's story nearly as significant as

Fitzgerald wants it to be. There is much in *Tender is the Night* which is moving and memorable: the decline of Diver, particularly, is beautifully done, despite the fact that we are never sure exactly what it is he is supposed to be declining from. Diver's increasing moodiness, his failure of tact, his drinking, his outbursts of irascibility, are what they are supposed to be, the surrender of a personality to its own most inferior elements; and the surrender is described intensely from within, yet judged simultaneously from without, by a fine exactitude of the understanding. There is too a genuine nobility in the attempt which is made to understand and describe the sufferings of the mentally sick whom Diver treats: one remembers especially the schizophrenic woman, bandaged and helpless, the prey to hideous hallucinations, who tells Diver that 'There must be a reason for all this suffering,' and one remembers too Diver's silence, his inability to answer her. This is not to say that we believe at all in Diver as a potentially great psychologist gone to seed: that belongs too to the unsuccessful part of the book. The unsuccessful part of the book, in fact, is most of what is supposed to be positive in it; the grace of the Divers' life, the intelligence which is at work within the grace and which is eventually sacrificed for it.

What is said here about *Tender is the Night* can be extended, by implication, to most of Fitzgerald's work, from *The Beautiful and Damned* onwards. In that early novel Fitzgerald's attempts to imagine a life of elegance, ease and irresponsibility are obviously at war with his own deeper and more serious wish, which seems scarcely confessed even to himself, to tell some kind of truth about marriage. At its worst the Fitzgerald hunger for glamour and prestige could lead to a passage like this, from an essay called *My Lost City*:

> 'The first speak-easies had arrived, the toddle was *passé*, the Montmarte was the smart place to dance and Lillian Tashman's fair hair weaved around the floor among the enliquored college boys. The plays were *Declassée* and *Sacred and Profane Love*, and at the Midnight Frolic you danced elbow-to-elbow with Marion Davies and perhaps picked out the vivacious Mary Hay in the pony chorus. . . .'

This is the language, and the life, one feels, of some third-rate BBC programme telling us that 'Those Were the Days' or 'The Lights Still Shine in Piccadilly' or whatever it is that those programmes are called; and yet it is about just this life that in the same essay Fitzgerald assures us, 'I had everything I wanted and knew I would never be so happy again.'

My conviction, as I have already indicated, is that when Fitzgerald was dancing among the 'enliquored college boys' he did *not* have 'everything he wanted'—that, rather, is something Fitzgerald would have liked to believe about himself, but never could. And when we turn to *The Last Tycoon*, the work he was busy on at the time of his death, we can see how much further Fitzgerald could go in trying to imagine for himself a desirable life. What makes Stahr heroic in Fitzgerald's eyes is clearly the fact that Stahr's is a working life: Stahr is involved, as all Fitzgerald's heroes are, with beauty, money and the manipulation of others for their own greater good, but these gifts or activities are all bent by Stahr to a single purpose. It is of course ironic and significant that the purpose is to make illusions, to make motion pictures; but the intention of the book is obviously to make Stahr not only the last tycoon he is declared to be in its title, but also a type of the artist. The artist and the business man are supposed to be antithetical figures, and in making the attempt to weld them into one Fitzgerald's ambition was as great here as it was in anything else he ever wrote. (And one should note in passing that it is hardly surprising that Fitzgerald himself should have ended up in Hollywood. Being the kind of man and artist he was, he was drawn inevitably towards it, and the attraction is evident as early as *The Beautiful and Damned*. Certainly he understood far earlier than most, perhaps because of his own attraction, what Hollywood was to become in the life of the nation and the world.)

He failed, however, with his tycoon-artist, just as he had failed earlier with Dick Diver to make meaningful and credible the interaction between the worlds of high fashion and profound intellect. We do not believe in Stahr, and I have already suggested that Fitzgerald's fundamental doubt about his own ability to depict the man is shown up by his use as narrator of the girl Celia, who is to Stahr what Rosemary was to Dick Diver. And the various other attempts made to inflate Stahr are sometimes dismaying in their crudity—there are, for example, the episodes involving Boxley, the English writer, who is shown as being contemptuous of all film-making, who is spoken to by Stahr, and who under Stahr's tuition subsequently takes over a writers' conference, having been made a new man by the words Stahr has said to him.

Obviously, it is unfair to criticize *The Last Tycoon* in this way, when Fitzgerald still had so much work to do on it; and I would not make the criticism if it did not seem to me that others have greatly over-praised the fragment which is all any of us have. I agree, certainly, that the fragment does have some notable strengths—the picture of Hollywood as a place where people actually work is unsurpassed; the natural aspect of California is beautifully, though fugitively, described; so too is the California of the boulevards and bungalows, the beaches and half-finished houses, drug-stores and parked cars; the love between Stahr and Kathleen is presented with all Fitzgerald's particularly effective wistfulness. And I agree too that for all the faults there are in his presentation, Stahr—who is a real aristocrat in a sense that none of Fitzgerald's other heroes are, for Stahr actually rules a kingdom of a kind—is the closest Fitzgerald ever came to making an adult embodiment of what he hoped or desired for himself and his society.

Nevertheless, it remains true, I believe, that all Fitzgerald's attempts at such an embodiment were failures, and marred each of his works, save for *The Great Gatsby*. *The Great Gatsby* is Fitzgerald's finest work precisely because in it he did not make any similar attempt.

The world of money, leisure and glamour in *The Great Gatsby* is represented by Tom Buchanan, his wife Daisy, and Daisy's friend, Jordan Baker. To their wealth they add sporting prowess, which was always of curious importance to Fitzgerald: Tom was 'one of the most powerful ends that ever played football at New Haven—a national figure in a way'; and Jordan Baker is a champion golfer. They live in immense style, having 'come East in a way that took your breath away'; but for once, in describing them, Fitzgerald's breath isn't taken away. The following passage, for example, may be compared with the quotation from *Tender is the Night* describing the Divers on the Riviera—this extract describes the narrator's entry into Tom Buchanan's house, and in its fluency, ease and freshness it is clearly superior to the other:

'We walked through a high hallway into a bright rose-coloured space, fragilely bound into the house by French windows at either end. . . . A breeze blew through the room, blew curtains in at one end and out the other like pale flags, twisting them up towards the frosted wedding-cake of the ceiling, and then rippled over the wine-coloured rug, making a shadow on it as the wind does on the sea.

'The only completely stationary object in the room was an enormous couch on which two young women were buoyed up as though upon an anchored balloon. They were both in white, and their dresses were rippling and fluttering as though they had just been blown back in after a short flight around the house. I must have stood for a few moments listening to the whip and snap of the curtains and the groan of a picture on the wall. Then there was a boom as Tom Buchanan shut the rear windows, and the caught wind died out about the room, and the curtains and the rugs and two young women ballooned slowly to the floor.'

Throughout the book the Buchanans are seen as being as much a part of their own expensive surroundings as the concluding phrases of the last sentence would suggest; and throughout they are described with the same rather contemptuous coolness. Because Fitzgerald makes it very plain, early in the book, that they are all contemptible people, without exception—Tom Buchanan with his crackpot racial theories and his vulgar amours; Jordan Baker who tells lies as a matter of course; even Daisy, with her beautiful voice, about which the narrator remarks, at their first meeting, 'The instant (it) broke off, ceasing to compel my attention, my belief, I felt the basic insincerity of what she had just said.' And as the book develops, these dishonesties and vulgarities develop too, until we see Daisy conspiring with her husband to use Gatsby's love for her

as a means of hiding her own guilt in the hit-and-run killing
of Myrtle Wilson; until we see Tom Buchanan deliberately
conniving at what he knows will be the murder of Gatsby.
There is no suggestion anywhere in the book that this leisure
class is 'truly brilliant and glamorous'; the members of this
class lead lives that are at best commonplace and at worst
sinister in a way that they themselves are too stupid to realize.

However, *The Great Gatsby* is very much more than an
'exposure', or a turning of the author upon himself. All
Fitzgerald's longing, nostalgia, wistfulness, all of what I have
called his hunger, are as much in this book as in any of his
others: indeed, even more so. But now Fitzgerald does not exert
himself in trying to make the object worthy of the hunger felt
for it: that, as I have shown is described as ash, as Dead Sea
fruit. No, the true emotional centre of the book is now in the
hunger itself: and its weight is that of the character of Gatsby.
In this respect, at least, Gatsby is treated without irony: the
book certainly uses Gatsby's hope, his 'heightened sensitivity
to the promises of life', for a profoundly ironic purpose; but it
could not have been used for that purpose if it had not been
given the respect and admiration which Fitzgerald obviously
feels for it, and which he persuades us it deserves. Gatsby is
described as a man 'with an extraordinary gift for hope, a
romantic readiness such as I have never found in any other
person and which it is not likely I shall find again'; and when
Gatsby at last meets Daisy again, after five years of waiting for
her, the admiration is made even more explicit. 'There must
have been moments that afternoon when Daisy tumbled short
of his dreams, not through her own fault, but because of the
colossal vitality of his illusion. It had gone beyond her, beyond
everything. He had thrown himself into it with a creative
passion, adding to it all the time, decking it out with every
bright feather that floated his way. No amount of fire or freshness,' the narrator continues, and he speaks for his creator too,
who is analysing here his own case, 'can challenge what a man
can store up in his own ghostly heart.'

To what extent Daisy does tumble short of Gatsby's dreams
the rest of the book reveals to us; and it is in this way that the
central irony of the book develops. 'They're a rotten crowd,'

the narrator shouts at Gatsby across the lawn, the last time he sees him. 'You're worth the whole damn bunch put together.' It is of course part of the irony that Gatsby, in his attempt to realize his 'incorruptible dream', should take to activities of a criminal nature—bootlegging, gambling, and, it is suggested more than once, murder. But the actual killers in the book, let it be noted, are Daisy and Tom Buchanan, though Daisy shrinks away from Gatsby when she is told about his past. Again, Gatsby may have a 'gonnegtion' with Meyer Wolfsheim, who 'fixed the World Series of 1919'; but about Jordan Baker, Daisy's best friend, the narrator remembers that 'at her first big tournament there was a row that nearly reached the newspapers—a suggestion that she had moved her ball from a bad lie in the semi-final round. The thing approached the proportions of a scandal—then died away. . . .' And so, throughout the book, the parallels are drawn, the connections are made, with a tightness, an unobtrusiveness, and an intelligence that are the mark of a liberated mind on the part of the creator: liberated because he is able to see himself for what he is, without hatred and without mercy; and to make of his own hatreds and compassion something that is no longer dependent upon himself for its life.

If the viciousness of the Buchanans is shown up against the 'incorruptibility' of Gatsby's dream, which has a nobility they cannot imagine; so, simultaneously, working in the other direction, Gatsby's dream is placed, tragically, not only by the means he has used to realize it, but by the fact that it is precisely around these wretched Buchanans that the dream coheres, it is towards them that it aspires. Tragic is a large word to use about so slender a book as *The Great Gatsby*, but I think it deserves it, if only because of the last great connection that is made in the novel: the connection between Gatsby and the country which had given him his birth. Fitzgerald's sense of history was acute (one of the finest scenes in *Tender is the Night* is that in which Dick Diver visits the trenches, 'where a century of bourgeois love died'); and in Jay Gatsby, Fitzgerald knew that he had created a character whose significance was not less than national. The passage with which the book concludes is so well known that one feels hesitant in quoting it, yet I cannot refrain from doing so—and not only because it illustrates so vividly and fully Gatsby's national or 'mythic'[1] aspect. At the end of *The Great Gatsby* the narrator stands outside Gatsby's mansion, and has a vision of 'the old island which flowered once for the Dutch sailors' eyes—a fresh green breast of the new world'.

> 'Its vanished trees (he continues), the trees that had made way for Gatsby's house, had once pandered in whispers to the last and greatest of all human dreams; for a transitory enchanted moment man must have held his breath in the presence of this continent, compelled into an aesthetic contemplation he neither understood nor desired, face to face for the last time in history with something commensurate to his own capacity for wonder.
>
> 'And as I sat there brooding on the old unknown world, I thought of Gatsby's wonder when he first picked out the green light at the end of Daisy's dock. He had come a long way to this blue lawn, and his dream must have seemed so close that he could hardly fail to grasp it. He did not know that it was already behind him, somewhere back in that vast obscurity beyond the city, where the dark fields of the republic rolled on under the night.
>
> 'Gatsby believed in the green light, the orgiastic future that year by year recedes before us. It eluded us then, but that's no matter—tomorrow we will run faster, stretch out our arms farther. . . And one fine morning——
>
> 'So we beat on, boats against the current, borne back ceaselessly into the past.'

The reader will surely have noticed the relevance of the entire quotation given above to the central argument or suggestion of this essay. In writing of the character of Gatsby and his country in this way Fitzgerald was writing too of himself; and only in this way did he succeed in doing himself full justice.

There are, it is true, certain criticisms to be advanced against the book, and in one of his letters Fitzgerald made perhaps the most important of these—that we are not told what

[1] The word is used by Mr Marius Bewley in his excellent essay on Fitzgerald in *The Eccentric Design*.

happened between Daisy and Gatsby after their reunion and before the climax of the book. I would also say that we are not told enough about Daisy's background when Gatsby meets her for the very first time and falls forever in love with her; nor enough about how Gatsby has made the money which he feels he needs before he can approach her again. It has been said that a novelist can withhold knowledge which he knows, and he can withhold knowledge which he does not know; and too often we feel that Fitzgerald's withholding in *The Great Gatsby* is of the second kind. However, I must say that none of these criticisms seem to me of any great significance. To speak quite simply, I would say that of all the American novels written since the first World War, which I have read, *The Great Gatsby* is the one I have read and re-read most often, and with the greatest pleasure.

Finally, there is one other aspect of Fitzgerald's achievement which must be mentioned. I think that any visitor to the United States must be surprised to find how curiously 'un-written-about' so much of the country seems to him, especially considering the great number of American novels which are continually being put out, and how many of them are little more than extended pieces of reportage. But to make any important feature of a country truly recognizable, one needs to do more than describe accurately particular physical appearances, or manners, voices, ways of speech; for the details of these things are somehow weightless and incoherent unless they are allied to a passionate preoccupation with the social depths which the details both reflect and imply. Fitzgerald's eye and ear were acute, and when he was fully engaged by his subject, as in *The Great Gatsby*, he was able fully to project his perceptions, in a way which, more than that of any other modern American novelist, helped to make the United States a country that not only is, but can be seen to be, a place of continuing habitation. Fitzgerald could not live in it, but others can, with greater understanding of themselves, because he tried to.

1960

ROBERT GRAVES AND THE
FIRST WORLD WAR

THERE ARE MANY REASONS why one should read, or reread, *Goodbye to All That*. On the simplest level the book is as informative and as continuously interesting as a good novel, whether it deals with the style of life of a cultivated literary family at the beginning of this century, or life in a public school before the first world war, or with Oxford just after the war; there is a curiously and disturbingly relevant chapter on Egypt as the author saw it when he served as a lecturer in English at the newly established university in Cairo. It can also be read as a document of the life of a poet whose influence on other poets, though never sensational, has been growing steadily, and some of whose poems are as likely to be read in fifty or a hundred years' time as any others the reader can think of. But, beyond these, there are reasons for reading *Goodbye to All That* which make its republication now particularly apposite, particularly an occasion for notice.

The book is quite justly most famous for its description of the fighting in the trenches of the first World War. If we think about such things at all today, we are so absorbed in the horrors of the last war, with its concentration camps and atomic bombs, and the threat of even more fantastic wars to come, that we forget what went before, what led up to the kind of world in which we live. But the trenches of the first world war are of our time: it is from them that our time has grown, with its anonymous and random slaughters, its own hysterias, its own precarious armistices. Robert Graves spares us none of the horrors of his war: the horrors of sight, smell and pain, and, over and above the others, the horror of the utter futility and meaninglessness of the suffering that the men in the trenches went through. In the trenches, as Graves describes them, there were no politics, not even in the way of hatred of the Germans (that was reserved for the French, and for those safe at home); there was no religion; there was no patriotism of a recognizable kind. There was only waste, disorder and death, in a nightmare that has its climax in the book at the description of a shambles of a 'dud show'—an offensive that ends in total disaster, and includes the indiscriminate gassing, shelling, and machine-gunning of Graves's regiment and several others by both British and German guns and gas companies.

Being what it is, telling the story that it does, *Goodbye to All That* is necessarily a book of anger and violent protest—and it is this not the less effectively for the control which the author uses over any expressions of anger or protest. Indeed, his control over his own feelings—and those of the reader—is so tight that the reader feels the outburst as a positive relief, when the news of the Armistice sends the author 'walking alone along the dyke above the marshes of Rhuddlan (an ancient battlefield, the Flodden of Wales) cursing and sobbing and thinking of the dead'. But the reader will notice that even here he is forbidden to indulge in his sense of relief: even here he is reminded of other battlefields and other wars than the one just ended.

This is not the only place in the book in which indulgence of any kind is forbidden to the reader. The absence of overt comment of a moralizing kind communicates to the reader a particular tension which is not the result of a mere literary device, but arises from the complexity of the attitude of the author towards his material. The war—as Robert Graves describes it—is unrelievedly futile and terrible; but the futility and the terror are never for a moment offered as an excuse for any failure of will or nerve on the part of the people with whom the author has to deal, or on the part of the author himself. When, on his first tour of the trenches, a group of men fail to salute him, and Graves writes, 'I thought this was a convention of the trenches . . . But I was wrong; it was just slackness,' we have here a very small example of the severity of tone which runs right through the book, and that finds its expression elsewhere in the author's intense pride in the traditions of his regiment, in his concern that the regimental record should be upheld, in his distaste for inefficiency, cowardice, or for that matter, stay-at-homes of almost any kind. The severity hardly ever becomes cold, hardly ever lacks compassion; the lapses into 'toughness' are very rare. In fact, it is the measure of the writing in the book that courage and order and the capacity for disciplined self-sacrifice become for the reader the standards by which it is possible to judge the foulness of the war, as they were once the standards by which it was possible for the author to go open-eyed through the war and yet retain—only just manage to retain—his sanity. His horror and his protest are unremitting; but they have their force because of the equally unremitting respect—indeed, the devotion—of the author to the stoic, soldierly virtues.

Goodbye to All That was written when the author was thirty-three, and was first published about as many years after the first World War as we are today distant from the Second. It seems to be the fashionable belief in England today that it is an easy matter for a writer to be angry and full of protest. The republication of *Goodbye to All That* after almost thirty years serves to remind us that true anger and true protest are as rare to find as they are desperately hard for an author to achieve. And as with figures so violently dissimilar in aims and achievement as Leavis, Orwell or Forster, what may look at first like eccentricity in Graves's approach is in fact what is most centrally, knottily, unyieldingly English in his work. It is something reassuring to encounter again, after one has heard some of the voices that claim to speak for England now.

1957

THE WRITER
IN THE COMMONWEALTH[1]

ON THE FACE OF it, it should be easy for me to discuss in general terms some of the literary problems or difficulties confronting the writer in the English language from the countries of the Commonwealth, being myself a writer from a country that until very recently was in the Commonwealth; and having as lively a sense of my own problems—being as quick to self-pity—as the next man. Allowing for the immense differences between the countries of the Commonwealth, it does seem to me that writers from each of these countries all have in common with one another certain problems which it may be useful to illustrate, and I hope, to illuminate.

But when one tries to define these problems, one finds oneself caught up in a welter of historical and quasi-literary speculation which very rapidly becomes unmanageable. Any literary discussion leads eventually from literature to questions of morals and ethics, to religion, to history, to sociology; even to geography, I am tempted to say in the present context. But in talking of writing from the colonial or Commonwealth countries one feels more than usually closely hemmed in by the extra-literary considerations which surround all literary discussion. And one feels this for a most disconcerting reason—simply, there is so little literature from these countries to talk about. There are no great, established instances around which the discussion can cohere, and from which those taking part in it

---

[1] This essay is a revised version of a talk originally given to the Doughty Society, Downing College, Cambridge.

can measure their distance at any point. It's gratifying to learn
that the English departments of at least two American universities, in Texas and Arkansas, have recently established
centres for the study of Commonwealth writing; nevertheless,
it remains true to say that in talking about Commonwealth
writing one is talking about a subject which does not truly
exist. Not yet, at any rate.

Perhaps I can make my point more clearly by pointing to
the analogy of the United States. In certain respects the experience in history of the US does resemble that of a country like
Australia, say, or even of South Africa. But the area in which
discussion of American writing can profitably take place has
been defined for us in the most profound and authoritative way
possible: it has been defined by the great American writers
themselves, who have established certain themes as being
characteristic of, or as standing in particular relationship to, the
patterns of American experience; it is they who have made
American experience available imaginatively to the American
people and to the rest of us.

We cannot say this about any 'Commonwealth writing' that I
am familiar with; not unless we make more allowances than our
own best hopes or ambitions should permit. Our points of
reference are scattered in isolation; and between them lies that
welter of generalization, a kind of bushveld through which it is
very difficult indeed to find one's way. All I can really do is to
strike directly into the bushveld, to try and describe some of the
general intellectual conditions which must govern literary
activity within the Commonwealth countries. Inevitably, my
descriptions are going to be schematic; and inevitably, too,
much of what I am going to say is autobiographical in nature,
though not in form.

I have referred to the 'intellectual conditions which must
govern literary activity within the English-speaking countries
of the Commonwealth'. What, in my own case, my upbringing
having been what it was and having taken place where it did,
do I feel to have been these governing conditions? What in my
intellectual environment as a South African was specifically
related to the country's past as a colonial settlement and its
status, until recently, within the Commonwealth? There are a

number of major conditions which can be baldly enumerated; they are all very closely interrelated: (1) the absence of a local literature; (2) the absence of any national intellectual tradition; (3) the absence of established and highly-developed social forms; (4) the absence of a local audience; and (5) the condition of exile—which is another way of describing the attractive power of the metropolitan country, of England. The list is rather a melancholy one, put down in this way, but I hope I will find something to say which will alleviate, if not entirely dissipate, the gloom which it might seem to portend.

The first condition I mentioned was *the absence of a local literature*; the fact that an English-speaking South African, to take my own example, grows up reading books which for the most part are from and about England; or from and about other countries; but hardly ever about South Africa. A consideration of the surprises, the difficulties, the tensions which are produced by this situation seems to me to lead directly into reflection on the whole nature of the literary activity as such; into reflection on the kind of recognitions and confirmations we seek from writing, both as writers and readers; the compulsions there seem to be upon us of naming the objects we see in the world around us, and of naming our own reactions to them; of enacting in words what we most wish for or fear. However, what I want to emphasize here is simply that for anybody with a literary bent who grows up under the circumstances I have mentioned, the consciousness of a gap or gulf between his reading and the world around him comes very early; it comes with his first nursery rhymes or learning-to-read books. And what those books begin, almost every other book he reads continues. When I think of the kind of book I read as a boy—the comics out of England, the 'William' books, books of a more meritorious nature—I know that I was continually and consciously trying to fit them against what I could feel and see in the world immediately around me; and often it was a very difficult task. The difficulty (and the necessity) of the task produces in one's attitude towards the books and towards the world around one a curious doubleness: it produces even in children what I am tempted to call an almost metaphysical preoccupation with 'reality'. Which was 'real'—the world of the books, or the world around one?

It is clear that one of the immediate intellectual consequences of the 'doubleness' could be to encourage the use of literature not to interpret the world which one inhabits oneself, but to escape from it. Strangely enough, it is possible to make the escape not only by exaggerating the differences between the world of books and the world one lives in, but also by denying that there are any differences at all; by insisting that 'there' and 'here' are one country, when they are nothing of the kind. In either case, what we have is an altogether inadequate notion of how closely grounded literature is in the society from which it emerges; and hence an insufficiently energetic conception of the relation between art and life, and what each can do or has done for the other.

But the 'doubleness' can have desirable consequences too, especially in the kind of training it can give in self-awareness. A South African or Australian who has any true perception of the complexity, variety, and richness of, say, the English literary tradition, is unlikely to deceive himself that he can simply imbibe the values of the tradition without effort, because of his birth into a particular family or class, or because of the school or university he attended. He knows that he has to work for a sense of the tradition, of its growth and modification through history, and it is possible that he will be more modest about what he has attained through his work than someone who is encouraged to believe that the tradition is available to him as a matter of social or historical right.

Much of what I have just said applies with equal force to the second of the governing conditions: *the absence of a national intellectual tradition*. I had thought of referring here simply to the absence of a sense of 'national identity'; but this seemed to me too narrow a description of what I have in mind. I can best illustrate what I mean by referring, again, to the analogy with the United States, which did develop, very early, its own traditions of moral and political thought. These traditions were certainly closely bound up with the problem of establishing a sense of national identity within the colonies and later in the republic; but it is clear that the American contribution to intellectual history cannot by any means be exhaustively defined in terms of that local problem. And it was in relation to these traditions (or in reaction against them) that the classic American novelists of the nineteenth century were able to pursue their individual preoccupations or obsessions. In South Africa, by contrast, there are no ideas, at once local and general, which could ratify, restrain, and objectify the competing nationalisms within the country; and it is partly for this reason that even at its best the intellectual life of the country has a haphazard, *extempore* quality about it, which often irritates the mind more than stimulates it, which encourages a kind of footloose eclecticism rather than a genuine creativity.

We have no literature, we have no intellectual tradition, in large measure simply because we have very few people, and those people have not been living long in their country.[1] And as a result of there having been so few people for so short a time in South Africa, the social fabric has a thinness, a simplicity, a tenuousness which it is difficult to describe, but which one must include in any enumeration of the conditions governing intellectual life in the country. It is this condition which I have called *the absence of established and highly-developed social forms*. We have all read that passage in Henry James's life of Hawthorne in which James compared, from the point of view of the novelist, English society with American; we remember 'the compassion' with which James was forced to regard 'a romancer' looking for subjects in the 'extraordinary blankness' of the American field. (Though we are inclined to forget that James went on to speak of the possibilities which yet remain for the American writer; they are, James wrote, 'his secret, his joke, as one might say'.) In any case, the 'denudation' of the social scene of which James complained can be seen in the society of a country like South Africa, with the further disadvantage I mentioned just a moment ago: the absence of a specific intellectual tradition comparable with that of the

[1] Even the Africans in South Africa have not been settled much longer in the country than the whites: in any case the tribal societies they had established have been all but destroyed over the last generation or two, and the Africans in the cities do give the impression, as much as the whites, of being an uprooted, newly-arrived people.

F

United States at the time James wrote, and of which James's *Hawthorne* is in itself most impressive evidence. The social tenuousness, the paucity of accepted social usages, is not something abstract, remote from one's everyday perception of the life around one. It might seem an exaggeration to say that one can hear an echo of it in the South African voice and accent, see a reflection of it even in the South African face; but in fact it is no exaggeration at all. And to think of this is to be reminded too of what I would call the imaginative flatness of the country's streets, of its buildings, even of its landscapes which seem merely to have been scratched and eroded, not developed and moulded, by the people who live among them.

But let us say that a South African, emerging from this society, writes a novel about it. Who will read his novel? Some South Africans will, certainly. But most of his audience will be in England or the United States: there is *no local audience* which is able to sustain him. To whom, then, is the South African novelist addressing himself? The answer is clear, if one looks at most South African novels. He is speaking to the people in London and New York. This mightn't seem to matter very much: after all, we read American novels, Russian, French, Japanese novels. But the novels from these countries were addressed by the novelists primarily to their own peoples; and this is one of their great strengths.[1] The novelist wanted to present to his own countrymen the people, the landscapes, the social classes, the intellectual impulses, with which they were already familiar, and which he wished to illuminate and re-define for them. The act of writing and the act of reading were conceived of, had to be conceived of, as a form of communion, a mutual exchange. But this it cannot be for the colonial novelist; at least not in the comparatively direct, straight-forward way it can be in countries which have audiences able to support and attend to their writers.

At the simplest level, the absence of a local audience encourages that wearisome explaining of local conditions by the

[1] The only exceptions I can think of are certain American novels, where one does find an ambiguousness about the audiences for whom they are intended. Cooper, for example, seems to write with one eye cocked across the Atlantic.

THE WRITER IN THE COMMONWEALTH

novelist (or poet) which on the one side becomes indistinguishable from the deliberate exploitation of local colour, and on the other side leads to prosy interpolations into the structure of the novel or poem. At another level we see colonial writers deliberately seeking for material which they imagine will be 'universal' in character; we see them trying to dissociate themselves from the very things in the scene immediately around them which should most be of concern to them. In all the cases referred to, the absence of a local audience to which the writer is answerable, first and last, produces in him the wrong sort of self-consciousness both about his audience and his subject-matter.

And the writers are inclined to gravitate, eventually, to the country they have always read about and where their books are most read. By doing so, they isolate themselves from the society which, however meagre and unsustaining they may have found it, is the only one they really know intimately; they attach themselves to the peripheries (or what they feel to be the peripheries) of a society which will always in some degree remain foreign to them. The gravitation to the metropolis is not something one can simply deplore; it seems to me to arise inevitably out of the circumstances I have previously described. The fifth governing condition which I mentioned earlier was *exile*.

I did say that I would try to dissipate something of the gloom my list of conditions would seem to threaten. It is obvious, however, that it is much easier to describe difficulties than it is to prescribe ways of overcoming them; especially when they are going to be overcome (if they are overcome at all) not through prescriptions but by examples—which, in the nature of the case, must be new and surprising, and must defy the prescriptions laid down for them.

Still, we always feel encouraged when we know that our difficulties are not as peculiar to ourselves as they sometimes seem to be; when we know that the problems we are faced with are not altogether unusual. What I have had to say about the situation of the Commonwealth writer seems to me to apply, *mutatis mutandis*, to the situation of the writer practically anywhere; and the disadvantages or disabilities under which the colonial suffers are not unlike those which handicap and stimulate his colleagues in England or the United States or elsewhere. For what appear to be difficulties may be described more optimistically, but not absurdly, as opportunities.

Consider 'exile'. Surely many of the greatest figures in modern literature have been, in a sense, exiles: Conrad, Eliot, Joyce, James, even Lawrence in the later years of his life. Exile certainly did not stultify their powers of creation. What was true of them may well be true even of lesser figures, both among those who live as outright exiles, and among those who feel themselves to be exiles, in some measure, within their own countries. Then, too, for a writer to come from anywhere in the Commonwealth to England, to the country I called simply 'the country he has always read about'—might that not in itself be a subject for the writer to ponder over, to work on, to use?

Is there any novelist today who writes with a firm sense of who his audience will be and what they will find familiar or unfamiliar in his work? Is the writer today not entitled to seek his community in terms other than those of locality and class; and is it not possible that if he devotes himself to his work, he will find that there will be others, of many races and in many places, who will be ready to perform their parts in the exchange which both sides are seeking? Under the assault of specialized knowledge of all kinds is there any of us who does not feel both intellectually disinherited and set free? Do we not all, under present-day conditions, need a measure of that self-awareness which I put forward as one of the most desirable consequences of a colonial education? Can the novelist in a 'new' society not find his material in the freedom of movement it offers to him, in the fluidity of its structure, the directness with which people in such a society reveal themselves to one another, the fierceness with which they seek their own identities? Is it not conceivable that the absence of comment upon the country around him, the absence of a recorded past within it, can in itself be a goad to the colonial writer, and can generate in him a creative excitement which he would not change for the excitements offered to other writers in other countries? And yet, at the same time, is not that excitement always a shared one, among all writers, for is it not true that every writer is always trying to describe people and a country which have never been described before— never as he has seen them, as he has imagined them?

We simply have to get on with the job; we have to make the best of what we have. That, at least, is no secret; no joke either.

1961

MARK TWAIN:

the Dandy and the Squatter

THE EARLIEST KNOWN WORK by Samuel Clemens is a short sketch called *The Dandy and the Squatter*, written when Clemens was sixteen years old and working as a printer on a village newspaper. The sketch describes an encounter between a 'spruce young dandy with a killing moustache &c., bent on making an impression on the hearts of some young ladies on board ship' and a 'tall, brawny woodsman' living in Clemens's own village, Hannibal. The dandy, who is a passenger on a steamboat passing through Hannibal, climbs off the boat and threatens the squatter, humorously: 'Say your prayers! . . . you'll make a capital barn door, and I'll drill the keyhole myself.'

> 'The squatter calmly surveyed him for a moment, and then, drawing back a step, he planted his huge fist directly between the eyes of his astonished antagonist, who, in a moment, was floundering in the turbid waters of the Mississippi. . . .'

The sketch is clearly of no literary merit. It can, however, be considered an extraordinary foreshadowing of the theme which was to occupy Mark Twain for most of his writing life: though to say this is to run the danger of serving all the most tired and jejune of the misconceptions about his work. The central misconception would be simply to identify Twain with the squatter and with his victory over the dandy; to imagine that Twain—the Westerner, the frontiersman—was to record in his books nothing but a series of backwoods victories over some or another kind of citified pretension or sophistication. The truth is, of course, a great deal more complicated; and even *The Dandy and the Squatter* is not without its own ambiguities and uneasiness. The sketch opens with the claim that Hannibal is 'now (a) flourishing young city', and the action of the story is set well into the past—'when such a thing as a steamboat was considered quite a sight'. But we know from *Life on the Mississippi* that at the time Clemens wrote his sketch Hannibal was hardly a 'city' of any kind, and that the arrival of a steamboat was even then still considered 'quite a sight' in the township. In other words, young Clemens is already trying to claim for himself and his town a degree of sophistication which they did not have; already he is doing his best to dissociate himself from the backwoodsman whose victory the sketch is supposed to be celebrating.

The uneasiness about the provincialism and vulgarity of his society, which Clemens revealed so clearly here, was characteristic of his literary predecessors, as Mr Kenneth Lynn shows in his very interesting study, *Mark Twain and Southwestern Humor*. The native writers whom Mr Lynn discusses were anxious to exploit for literary purposes the life immediately around them, and anxious too to explore the literary possibilities of vernacular speech. In their determination to remain gentlemanly and sophisticated, however, these writers always 'framed' in conventional narration the passages of vernacular writing which they permitted themselves. Twain was the first to abandon the convention altogether in *Huckleberry Finn*: he thereby set himself free to confront his characters and their society without the embarrassments which were to spoil so much else in his own work. By adopting totally (or seeming to adopt totally) the vernacular of the society he had come from, Twain was not surrendering to that society; on the contrary this was the condition of his freedom from either aggression or defensiveness in writing about it.

Every good book is a record of the author's war with himself: the critic has to be careful in taking sides, especially when he is dealing with someone as supple and as treacherous as Mark Twain, whose wars were all guerilla campaigns fought by armed bands wearing no uniforms and sharing no principles.

Twain was an extraordinarily complicated person; and it is impossible to read any account of his life—or to go through the two sumptuous volumes of the *Mark Twain—Howells Letters* which have recently been published—without feeling that all one's usual habits of summary and judgment are of little value here: the man escapes every time, even as one grasps at him. And it is evident that he escaped often enough from his own grasp, and went blundering pitiably into many kinds of disaster, both in his life and his work. One can say truthfully about him that he was at once a vulgarian and the victim of the worst gentilities of his time; that he debased his own gifts for the sake of money and applause; that he was a clown, a show-off, and a coward. But one says these things a little shamefacedly when one remembers that Twain was the first to say them about himself, and not in any self-pitying way, but in pain and sincerity. And one's appetite for moral certitudes diminishes even further when one remembers, too, that Twain's aspirations to live better and work better produced not another *Huckleberry Finn*, but instead (and this is a measure of the complexity of the case) an unreadable book like *The Personal Recollections of Joan of Arc*.

In the end, after a public success comparable to that of Charles Dickens, Twain despaired—despaired of life, of art, of himself. ('Why *was* the human race created?' Twain wrote to Howells in a characteristic note, 'Or at least why wasn't something creditable created in place of it? God had His opportunity; He could have made a reputation. But no, He must commit this grotesque folly.') Twain's 'pessimism' has been ascribed to his bankruptcy after the failure of his lunatic business adventures, which was followed immediately by the death of his beloved daughter, Susie; it has been regarded as the punishment visited upon him by his thwarted, abused artistic conscience; it has also been hailed—rather simple-mindedly I believe—as a sign of the depth of his insight into the human condition. 'Bile! give me more bile; fry me an optimist for breakfast,' he wrote; and yet he timed his appearances in Fifth Avenue so that he would catch the crowds, and he wore a dazzling white suit to make sure the crowds wouldn't miss him. No wonder almost every American critic who has written about Twain has chosen to write of his life as an allegory of the Artist in America; and certainly there is a curious, almost frightening resonance between Twain's empty, enraged success and the silence and anonymity of Melville.

It would be wrong, however, to leave the emphasis there. A sense of waste and frustration is inevitable when one reads widely in Mark Twain's works; but the qualities which make *Huckleberry Finn* a great book are to be found sporadically, erratically, in many of his other works. *The Innocents Abroad, Life on the Mississippi, A Connecticut Yankee in King Arthur's Court, Pudd'nhead Wilson, Tom Sawyer,* as well as the strange, late, Hawthorne-like moral fables, *The Man Who Corrupted Hadleyburg* and *The Mysterious Stranger*—all these have sustained passages which show how prodigious was Twain's talent, how remarkable was his capacity to tell the truth. Admittedly, one has to exercise patience in seeking these passages out. In *The Innocents Abroad,* for example, one sometimes feels that when Twain isn't trying to blow the gaff on Europe and all its art and culture, he is trying to show that if it pleases him he can be just as 'sensitive' and 'poetic', too, as the next travel-writer. So the writing alternates between jeers and purple-patches—except at those times when Twain asks himself, sincerely, 'What do I really see here? What do I really feel about it?' And without fuss or pretension, with a calm, profound honesty, he answers his own questions: he sees a great deal, he feels deeply about it, and he is able to describe the external scene and his own reaction to it fluently and finely. These moments of stillness give *The Innocents Abroad* its true life; in *Huckleberry Finn* a similar stillness prevails almost throughout the book. This stillness, the unwavering purity of Huck's honesty, is the medium through which we perceive all the movement and violence of the action.

About *Huckleberry Finn* there are two further points to be made. The first is that in this book Twain—who was to describe his own views on mankind as 'ordure'—succeeded as very few other novelists have, and certainly as no other American novelist has, in drawing a totally convincing picture of human goodness. Both Huck and Jim are good; and their goodness is not a matter of assertion on the author's part, but arises spontaneously from what they are and what they do: it is the very sap of the book drawn from its deepest levels and carrying life to every scene which the boy and the Negro participate in or witness. (Except for the last chapters, where Tom Sawyer is dominant, and the truth of the book has been lost.) The goodness of Huck and Jim sets in relief the wickedness of so much of the life on the river's banks, and the brutal falsity of the King and the Duke who take over the raft; but, as Professor Lynn points out in his criticism of the book, Huck and Jim are not set in simple opposition to the people around them. Huck is forced to exercise his goodness precisely because he had so much that is false within himself, and because his status as an outcast carries with it its own moral dangers, as the fate of his father testifies. Huck is entitled to judge the evil to which so much of the society has succumbed precisely because he so many times almost succumbs to it himself.

The second point to be made arises directly out of the first. It is important that we should not take Huck's explicit views on 'sivilization' ('I can't stand it. I been there before') as the last, nostalgic summation of the book. If the sojourn on the raft were no more than an escape, no more than a threatened idyll—as it is so often considered to be—*Huckleberry Finn* would be very much less interesting than it is. By any definition of the word, the relationship between Huck and Jim on the river is considerably more 'civilized' than any relationship which they can enjoy with anyone else or with each other, on the shore. The relationship between the two on the raft demands from them both the sacrifices which civilization demands from us all, and which we frequently find most burdensome to make: it demands mutual responsibility, self-abnegation, and moral choice. Whatever else he may be, Huckleberry Finn is no ancestor of the Beat Generation. The tragedy of the book is that the fineness of Huck's relationship with Jim is impermanent; it cannot survive on shore, as the last chapters dismally demonstrate. Though he did not realize it, this is the saddest and fullest judgment that Twain was ever to make of 'the damned human race'.

1960

OUT OF AFRICA

FROM MANY QUARTERS TODAY one hears the expression of a hope, an expectation, even a demand: out of emerging Africa a literature must come.

Why should it? one can't help asking, a little sullenly.

Because Africa is emerging, comes the irritated reply. Can't you *see* that Africa is emerging?

Indeed, one can. But what makes people think that they are entitled so soon and so easily to ask of Africa that it produce nothing less than a literature? Before making their demands, shouldn't they ask what Africa is emerging out of, and what it is emerging into, and *then* see how much they may reasonably hope for in the way of literature? And shouldn't they ask, anyway, what they mean by Africa? 'Africa' isn't a place or a country, but a huge and multifarious continent—so huge and multifarious that no generalization that one makes about it can possibly be true. Not even the generalization that it is 'emerging'.

Still, let us say that it (whatever 'it' is) *is* emerging. Now what is it emerging from? What is the past that the writer in Africa has to draw upon? And let us remember that a writer is as dependent on the past as he is on the future: he can write most meaningfully only when there is a past to which he can refer, just as he can write meaningfully only when he is convinced that there is going to be a future in which his work will in turn be part of the past. 'It takes a great deal of history to produce a very little literature': this may be of small comfort to those who believe that every publisher's list every spring and autumn must contain its quota of 'literature'; but it is true. And there is a sense in which, in a literary context, one can say that

Africa has had a very short history indeed; that its history begins with the invasion of the continent by the white man.

We must not be confused by the political term 'Afro-Asian' into imagining that Africa and Asia are alike; they are not; or at least they are as much different as they are alike. Asia is emerging from a state of comparative technical backwardness, but India, China, Ceylon, Burma, and the rest are countries with high, ancient, and complex civilizations (and high, ancient and complex literatures) behind them and within them. Can we say the same about South Africa? About Rhodesia? About Tanganyika? About Sierra Leone and Gambia?

Obviously not. In the countries of Africa (south of the Sahara, at any rate) the penetration of the West has never been an interpenetration with the kind of civilization that has existed for so many hundreds and even thousands of years in Asia. 'Mankind remembers the history of peoples,' writes Hannah Arendt, in *The Burden of Our Time*, 'but has only a legendary knowledge of prehistoric tribes . . . What made them (the Africans) different from other human beings was not at all the colour of their skin but the fact that they behaved like a part of nature, that they had not created a human world, a human reality, and that therefore nature had remained, in all its majesty, the only overwhelming reality—compared to which they appeared to be phantoms, unreal and ghostlike.'

Now I know it will be said that recent archaeological researches have shown that in the past of West Africa, if not elsewhere in the continent, there was a much greater 'human reality' than the first white explorers and traders managed to see. But, in the present context, these archaeological researches seem much less significant than the liberals among the whites and some of the politicians among the blacks would try to make them out to be. The 'human reality' of a civilization is a reality only if there is some continuity to it, only if it is present in the consciousness of the people as a force controlling, guiding, and inspiring them, in a way that they themselves are aware of. But in most of Africa, whatever formal civilizations there may have been seemed to have lapsed almost entirely out of the consciousness of the race. It does not really matter whether the tribes (to quote Miss Arendt again) 'represent "prehistoric

man", the accidentally surviving specimens of the first form of
human life, or whether they are the "posthistoric" survivors of
some unknown disaster which ended a civilization . . . They
certainly appeared rather like the survivors of one great catastrophe which might have been followed by small disasters,
*until catastrophic monotony seemed to be a natural condition of human
life*' (my italics).

This, I suggest, is what the largest part of Africa is emerging
out of; and I suggest too that it is a 'past' which for obvious
reasons is peculiarly difficult for the African writer to conduct
into his present work as a fertilizing and invigorating influence.
The difficulties can hardly be enumerated, they are so great;
but they can be illustrated by mentioning the single fact that
most Africans who want to write choose to do so in English or
French, rather than in their native languages. Could there be,
for a writer, a more dramatic sign of a severance from the past
than his adoption of a language other than the one spoken by
his people in their own past? And in adopting this other
language, is he not immediately putting himself into an awkward
and problematical relationship with his people in their present?

As for the present, from the point of view of literary expectation, as for what Africa is emerging into, let me offer another
depressing quotation, this time from W. B. Yeats. 'How small a
fragment of our own nature can be brought to perfect expression,
nor that even but with great toil, in a much divided civilization.'

Our civilization isn't merely divided, it's distraught. And
imagine, say, England with little in it that wasn't knocked up
hastily within the last fifty years or so, and at the same time
poorer than it was before the Industrial Revolution; imagine
it racked with nationalism and racial problems, imagine it
largely illiterate *and* (this is the point) already equipped complete with the *Daily Mirror* and *Reveille*, with Hollywood films
and strip-cartoons; and ask yourself how much literature, under
such circumstances, England could be expected to produce.
And actually there is no need to imagine such catastrophes
overwhelming England: it isn't as though literature is exactly
flourishing in this country today. It is thirty years since
Lawrence died; twenty years since the death of Yeats; and

F**

how much has England to show of major work since then?

But it would merely be folly to go on to say, 'What a world to emerge into!' or 'How much better the Africans would be if they would stay out of it!' The Africans are emerging into this world; and they want as much of the things this world offers as they can get. Everyone wants enough food, a house of brick rather than a house of mud, and a motor-car too, if he can get one; and our civilization can produce food and houses and motor-cars, if it can do nothing else. But I think that one can say, without exaggeration or self-pity, that it isn't a civilization propitious towards the growth and sustenance of a literature.

But I am not trying to suggest that no good writing can come out of Africa.

Actually, all I have been anxious to do is simply to assert in a small way, and in an area which I feel to be near to me, the autonomy of literature. I believe that to link too closely together our literary expectations with our political or nationalist expectations is positively dangerous. It is dangerous to literature directly and obviously, in the way of patronage, bullying, and censorship; and it is no less dangerous indirectly because of its effect on the life out of which literature comes. Politics today is an omnivorous activity; it would gladly swallow literature whole; and in trying to prevent this we are holding out against the tendency of politics in our time to turn us all into its servants, to leave us no room for private manoeuvre, private ambition, private love, private life. This is a ubiquitous tendency; it reached its fullest expression (so far) in the totalitarianisms of Hitler and Stalin; and we are all in one way or another given to helping it along, even when we least know that that is what we are doing. And the liberal expectation that a politically emerging Africa should promptly produce a literature to match, the liberal determination to find such a literature even if it does not exist, seems to me a part of this tendency. A small part, perhaps an unimportant part; certainly a well-intentioned part; but a deplorable one nevertheless.

I hope it is possible to write in this way without being accused of being an 'aesthete' or the inhabitant of an ivory tower. If one cares in any sane or useful way about writing, one certainly cares a great deal about politics, and the relation between the two. Given a fair chance, literature will meet and make use of politics and nationalism, and be of use to them, just as she will meet anything else human. Think of what participation in the Irish nationalist movement did for the poetry of Yeats. Think of what the sentiment of national consciousness has been in the literature of Russia, or that of the United States; or for that matter, the literature of the Boers in South Africa. But the point is that politics nowadays 'gives' nothing its fair chance; the chance has to be fought for, everywhere, all the time.

Throughout I have been talking as though the 'African' writer is necessarily black; but of course he need not be. And it is only fair to both the black and the white writer in Africa to add that what I have had to say about the black seems to me to apply even more forcefully, though under somewhat different circumstances, to the white. The white writer is a member of a society which has no roots in the past, or no past at all; his present, so far as it is stable, is tawdry, vulgar and thin, and, so far as it is in movement, is without any security whatsoever; he is cut off from the surge to political power that is animating the African consciousness in its every aspect.

It seems quite possible to me that if a worthwhile and recognizable African literature should emerge, it might be of a kind that will surprise and disappoint some of those who are most eagerly looking forward to its appearance. For I see no way for the African writer but to make his matter out of his handicaps, his disadvantages, his disabilities. There is a sense of course in which every writer does this[1]; but when the disadvantages are of the kind that seem to confront the African writer, he will need a boldness and a toughness of a rather special kind.

Out of the loneliness and the sense of deracination I foresee

[1] Mr V. S. Naipaul's remarkable novel, *A House for Mr Biswas*, which is set in Trinidad, seems to me very much a case in point here. The hero of that book is starved and frustrated at every turn by the 'colonial' nature of his society; just because the society is so unsparingly anatomized for us, we are able to appreciate how striking is the hero's achievement in never being entirely defeated by it. Even his own perception of what he has been deprived of is shown to be a kind of victory over the most discouraging social and cultural circumstances.

him suffering, I cannot believe that a writing of easy affirmation can come. His affirmation will be in the effort he has made; and if he tries truly then others will be encouraged to go on trying too. For in making or postulating for himself his own past, in projecting in his work the society he hopes will one day attend to him, he will be doing what any serious writer nowadays has to do.

Whether or not Africa will produce such writers we cannot say. When it does, it will have emerged—even if it then treats them no better than America once treated Melville, or Russia now treats Pasternak.

1959

DOWN THE RIVER

'IS THERE ANYTHING GLORIOUS and dear for a nation that is not also glorious and dear for a man? What is freedom to a nation, but freedom to the individuals in it? What is freedom to that young man who sits there, the tint of African blood on his cheeks, its dark fires in his eyes? . . . To your fathers, freedom was the right of a nation to be a nation. To him, it is the right of a man to be a man, and not a brute; the right to call the wife of his bosom his wife, and to protect her from lawless violence; the right to protect and educate his child; the right to have a home of his own, a religion of his own, a character of his own, unsubject to the will of another.'

These thoughts, Harriet Beecher Stowe tells us, were 'rolling and seething' in the breast of a runaway slave, George Harris, as he waited to cross the border between slavery in the United States and freedom in Canada. What thoughts, one wonders, are rolling and seething (if those are the words) in the breast of the Negro student who, exactly a hundred years after Lincoln proclaimed the liberation of the slaves in the United States, today goes about the campus of the University of Mississippi, protected by a squad of Federal Marshals? It is a melancholy reflection on the present state of affairs that it is quite impossible to read *Uncle Tom's Cabin* with any measure of detachment. As we go through the book we are forced to ask ourselves repeatedly whether it can still tell or teach us anything—not only about the United States, but about ourselves; about all of us who in some way or another cannot help responding positively to Mrs Stowe's rhetoric.

I am not sure whether we can learn more from the book's faults than from its merits; but I am sure, at least, that we can learn something from our own misguided insistence, over these last many years, that the book has no merit at all. As Mr Edmund Wilson has written recently, in his study of the literature of the American Civil War, *Patriotic Gore*, 'To expose oneself in maturity to *Uncle Tom* may prove a startling experience. It is a much more impressive work than one has ever been allowed to suspect.' Chief among the reasons which Mr Wilson gives for this judgment is what he calls the 'eruptive force' of the novel: the vitality with which the characters come before us, 'lamenting and ranting, prattling and preaching'; the variety and verisimilitude of the descriptions of the homes and farms in which the characters live, the steamboats on which they travel, the slave-markets at which they are sold; the comedy of the contrasts in manners between New Englanders and Southerners, slavetraders and Quakers. But what is most unexpected in the book, Mr Wilson goes on to say, 'is that, the farther one reads in *Uncle Tom*, the more one becomes aware that a critical mind is at work, which has the complex situation in a very firm grip and which, no matter how vehement the characters become, is controlling and co-ordinating their interrelations.' Throughout the book a resolute attempt is made to apportion credit and blame fairly between Southerners and Northerners for the conditions under which the slaves live, to distinguish between all the varying shades of Southern practice and opinion on the question, and to make it plain that legislation alone will not solve the terrible problem which greed, cruelty and lack of imagination has saddled the country.

To this one must add that from the very first page the novel shows an exhilarating and (to us) astonishing confidence in its own form—though to speak of 'form' in connection with a book written in such a pell-mell, haphazard manner may seem a contradiction in terms. Mrs Stowe was not inhibited by any anxiety about 'points of view', 'unity of action', 'impersonality' or any other abstract, literary consideration; she had no doubt about her right to speak up for her characters during their moments of silence, to pontificate about them, to take the reader by the sleeve and coax, hector and shame him into agreement with her. Scandalous though this way of going about things may at first seem, we are forced by it to realize, as we read on, just how much our idea of what a novel is capable of doing has dwindled over the last century—which, among other things, is a way of saying that we realize how little confidence we now have in our own moral passions. The novel's 'eruptive force', its apparent formlessness, and its author's total moral certitude are all inseparable from one another; each is an aspect of the others.

But why is it, then, that for so many years we have been unable to read *Uncle Tom*? For the ironic fact is that this novel, which was written by Mrs Stowe to hearten and inspire the 'liberals' and 'progressives' of her day, and to shame the reactionaries, has ended up as a source of embarrassment and ridicule to the liberals of our own. The book has been mocked and parodied in a thousand ways; Mr James Baldwin has written a passionate essay denouncing it and its influence on all other 'protest' novels; I can remember, years ago, hearing a radical friend at the university in Johannesburg describing *Cry the Beloved Country* as 'South Africa's *Uncle Tom's Cabin*', and I can remember, too, our complete conviction that with this phrase both books had been neatly and finally disposed of. Most damning to it of all, perhaps, is that it has become an insult to speak of a Negro as 'an Uncle Tom': he has become the archetypical figure of the black man who is incapable of resisting his own enslavement; of any grateful, self-sacrificing, praying, obsequious creature who loves his masters and is loved by them precisely because he is so much less than a man, and never tries to become one. When Tom is sold down the river he turns down a chance to run away: 'Mas'r always found me on the spot—he always will. I never have broke trust . . . and I never will.' When he is sold once again to St Clare: 'Tom looked up . . . (He) felt the tears start in his eyes as he said heartily, "God bless you, mas'r".'

If we are moved at all by such passages, it is likely to be to scorn at Tom and anger at the author who holds him up to our admiration. And then there are all those pages of odious moralizing in the book, and its flights of rhetoric; there is the pornographic zeal with which Mrs Stowe starts working herself up, over a distance of many chapters, towards the death of Little Eva; there is the awful archness of much of the humour; there are those descriptions of Negro mothers being torn away from their children which Mrs Stowe lingers over with an ugly, unconscious pleasure; there are the innumerable condescending references to the Negroes as 'the childlike race', 'the impressionable race', 'the simple race'; there is that interminable procession of stock 'darkies' whose antics are intended to raise a smile we are quite unable to give. Taking all this into account, I admit it is very easy to see why *Uncle Tom* has been regarded as a book to weep over in one's childhood, and then to put firmly out of mind—except as a warning against the consequences of indulging in uncontrolled spasms of piety and patronage.

However, I don't believe that these criticisms altogether explain the violence with which the book has been condemned, or the way in which its complexities and strengths have been overlooked. *Uncle Tom's* sentimentality may be odious, but it is not any more so than many other nineteenth-century classics which adults are not ashamed to be found reading. Mrs Stowe's rhetoric does not seem to me really very much more objectionable than William Faulkner's, say; and it has the advantage over much of Faulkner's in being comprehensible. Moreover, the book describes the adventures of George and Eliza Harris, as well as those of Uncle Tom; and George and Eliza *do* defy their masters, they do 'break trust' and run away, and as a result are rewarded by gaining their freedom and being re-united with one another; George is subsequently given an education at a university in France. Indeed, considering how richly rewarded George is for his defiance, and what disasters overtake Tom as a result of his obedience, I am a little surprised that no one has had the idea of making a Lawrencian reading of the book, and finding in it a moral quite opposite to the one Mrs Stowe imagined she was pointing. ('You *must*,' Lawrence wrote, 'look through the surface of American art, and see the diabolism of the symbolic meaning.')

Such a reading is not one that I myself actually believe it

necessary to make. For the truth is that, despite all the pages
devoted to demonstrating his implausible fidelity to his masters,
even Tom is not quite the character he is usually supposed to
be. In the end, Tom, too, does defy a white man—the most
brutal and dangerous of them all.

> ' "And now," said Legree, "come here, you Tom. You see, I
> telled ye I didn't buy ye jest for the common work; I mean
> to promote ye, and make a driver out of ye; and tonight ye
> may jest as well begin to get yer hand in. Now, ye jest take
> this yer gal and flog her; ye've seen enough on't to know
> how."
>
> ' "I beg mas'r's pardon," said Tom; "hopes mas'r won't set
> me at that. It's what I an't used to—never did—and can't
> do, no way possible." '

Tom persists in his refusal to be 'promoted' in this way; and as
a direct result he is himself eventually flogged to death.

Tom dies in hope of gaining a heaven which few liberals or
radicals today believe in. This has made it a great deal easier
for us to reject Tom and all we have chosen to believe he
stands for. But, given the nature of his ultimate defiance, and
given the care which Mrs Stowe has taken to implicate all her
characters (and all her readers) in the conditions which permit
a man like Legree to have unqualified power over the lives of
others, one cannot help wondering if our revulsion from Tom
doesn't spring in part from an uneasy fear that his way of
asserting his humanity might be as effective as any other way
open to him—or to us. Despite all that has happened in
America and everywhere else, over the last hundred years, we
persist in hoping that there is some forceful, simple, final way of
winning or giving to others the freedom of which Mrs Stowe
wrote in the first paragraph quoted above; we persist in hoping
that the Federal marshals—or whatever their equivalent might
be elsewhere—will be able to impose human brotherhood upon
us, once and for all, and thus relieve us of the necessity of making
any solitary or even apparently hopeless efforts of our own.
Mrs Stowe did not share in this delusion; nor did the hero of
her novel. It does not seem to me to be impugning the dignity
of the Negro students and passive resisters in the Deep South

to say that their actions have something in common with Uncle Tom's.

Perhaps the worst thing about *Uncle Tom's Cabin* is that Mrs Stowe never fully imagined that the day would come when Negroes would read her novel and comment on it; she never appeared to have asked herself what her university-educated George Harris, for example, would have made of all her 'kindly' references to his race, or of Uncle Tom's martyrdom, or of her compulsion to make both George himself and Eliza as 'white' in appearance as she possibly could. In view of the cause she was pleading, this failure of imagination is obviously a crucial one; and one for which she is less and less likely to be forgiven in the future. However, we can trust her sufficiently to say that she would not have minded this at all.

1962

FRANZ KAFKA:

A Voice from the Burrow

IN SPEAKING OF FRANZ KAFKA, it is as well to speak of him
first as a Jew, because in doing so one is able to arrive at an idea
of the extreme, the crippling, degree of isolation and alienation
from which he suffered as a man and an artist. Commentators
on Kafka have often written as though the relation between
Kafka's Jewishness and his sense of his own isolation were a
simple and self-evident one; but this seems to me to betray an
inadequate notion of what was amiss with Kafka himself, and
an altogether external notion of what it means to be a Jew.

Kafka was born of bourgeois parents in Prague; his father was
a crass, conventional man on whose shoulders Kafka was later
to lay the blame for his personal inadequacies and failures;
Kafka's mother was descended from a distinguished rabbinical
family. The family observed the customs of Orthodox Judaism,
not so much out of belief apparently, as out of conventionality.
Kafka attended synagogue regularly as a child; his lifelong
friend, Max Brod, who was to become his biographer, was a
devoted Zionist; and in the last few years of his life Kafka returned to the study of Hebrew and the Talmud. It has often
been remarked that the 'dialectic' of the Kafka fable has
unmistakable affinities with the characteristic methods of
Talmudic exegesis; and his humour, too, has been considered
to be typically Jewish, in its irony, tenacity, and self-depreciation.

All this may well be true; but whether we consider Judaism
as a formal religion, or 'Jewishness' as the vague but potent
fusion of convention, habit, family loyalty, and community

feeling it so often is, we cannot but be struck by how positively 'un-Jewish' is the spirit of Kafka's work. Judaism, as a religion, is essentially normative; of all religions it is the one which sets most store by direct unambiguous commandments, governing not only religious observances and ethics, but also the minutiae of everyday living. And in the Jewish tradition, the study of the Law, as it has been revealed, is the highest activity open to man. I believe that in writing, as he so often did, of a man who is found guilty of a crime he did not commit, under a law he is ignorant of, Kafka was expressing symbolically, among many other things, his own sense of being profoundly sundered from the tradition in which he had been brought up. The inversion of Judaism, so to speak, cannot be accidental.

Again, if we are to talk of 'Jewishness' merely, it seems clear that in their very isolation, their absence of antecedents, families or friends, Kafka's heroes are not recognizably Jews at all. To be a Jew is certainly to know social unease, under the best conditions, and to face appalling dangers and degradation under the worst; but the isolation this involves is of a very different kind from that suffered by Kafka's heroes. If we say that as a Jew, or because he was a Jew, Kafka knew loneliness and powerlessness, we are saying only that he knew all the disadvantages but none of the very real advantages of being a Jew—neither the authority and stability of the Jewish Law, nor the common, human, frail satisfactions of simply being Jewish.

But then what did Kafka know or show in his work of stability of any kind; what did he know of the common, frail advantages of simply being human? To ask this question as if it were a reproach may seem to show very little charity to a man who suffered greatly in his life, and who was able to embody that suffering in works which I have no doubt will remain of permanent interest. Nevertheless, the question must be asked, if only because during the vogue for his work, some years ago, so many people were ready to hail him as the voice of modern Europe—a claim which it seems to me cannot possibly be sustained. In Kafka's work there is nothing of the world of nature, nothing of the delight of the senses, nothing of love, of family affection, of friendship. It might seem as though this is to condemn Kafka simply because his work is too 'gloomy' or 'pessimistic', but that is not the point at all. On the contrary, it can be as parents and children, husbands and wives, that we can suffer most deeply; we can come to know our own impotence because of our perception of the indifference of the natural world outside ourselves; it is because our senses can feel delight that they can feel pain too. But of these pains Kafka can tell us as little as he can of their complementary or concomitant pleasures. He simply knew too little about them.

And not only was his knowledge extremely limited; he was incapable of even trying to learn more. As incapable, in fact, as any of his heroes ever are of trying to move away from the various kinds of imprisonment in which they find themselves, or of protesting against the malice of the authorities who confine them, or of destroying themselves sooner than allowing themselves to be destroyed. In *The Castle* the hero is enjoined to leave the village, where he is being endlessly tormented by the staff on the castle hill. But,

' "I can't go away," replied K. "I came here to stay. I'll stay here." And giving utterance to a self-contradiction which he made no effort to explain, he added as if to himself, "What could have enticed me to this desolate country except the wish to stay here?" '

Exactly; and it is just this wish, or rather, the fact that he is incapable of wishing for anything else, even momentarily, which makes him so unrepresentative a hero. In *The Trial* Joseph K. says explicitly to the Examining Magistrate that the trial is one only as long as he, Joseph K., recognizes it as such. 'But for the moment,' he adds, 'I do recognize it'; and he does not cease to do so throughout the book.

The Trial opens with the sentence: 'Someone must have been telling lies about Joseph K., for without having done anything wrong he was arrested one fine morning.' Now anyone thinking of Kafka as a twentieth-century Jew must reflect, when he reads this, that the sentence is almost literally true to what happened during the years of the Nazi hegemony in Europe to almost six million living individuals. Someone had indeed been telling lies about them, and as a result they were taken away to meet fates as gruesome, or more so, as that meted out to Joseph K. at the end of the book. But these people, unlike Joseph K., were not self-condemning solitaries. What is most dreadful about their fate, what one cannot even begin to comprehend about it, is that they were perfectly ordinary people, with families and hopes, fears and ambitions for themselves; and what was done to them was done in the days and nights that lit or darkened the same commonplace world of everyone who was living at that time. Kafka's tale cannot encompass the horror at all; his book is too private, too small, too exclusive an affair altogether.

Admittedly, this is an extreme case: what work of art can measure up to the demented horrors of Hitler's Europe? But I have made the case because I believe it to show up clearly how little Kafka can be said to speak for Europe, even its most tormented aspect. Dostoevsky may have been a hateful man, and as diseased as Kafka in his private life; but if we set against any of Kafka's fables the fable of 'The Grand Inquisitor' from *The Brothers Karamazov*, we have to grant Dostoevsky a kind of nobility as a writer which Kafka is altogether without. Dostoevsky's fable has the nobility of true protest, of true rebellion, of a spirit trying to beat through the walls of its own limitations, instead of merely walking around within the walls and examining them minutely, fanatically, even lovingly, having lost all hope of reaching the world outside itself.

The most one can say about Kafka is that his fidelity to the nature of his own experience is astonishing; and all the more so when one considers the form in which he chose to record it. In the volume, *Descriptions of A Struggle*, which concludes the publication of the English definitive edition of his works, there are gathered together fables, pieces and aphorisms of varying lengths, dealing with such different topics as the confusions to be found among the builders of the Great Wall of China, the claustral anxieties of a beast who digs a burrow for itself under the ground and then begins to suspect that a bigger animal is doing the same thing elsewhere in the burrow, the speculations of a dog as to where his food really comes from, the embarrass-ments of an elderly bachelor who finds himself accompanied by two little bouncing balls wherever he goes. Given the

arbitrariness and caprice of the form, one might have imagined
that Kafka would have been tempted to do anything with it;
but all he does is to delineate and define the terms of his own
imprisonment. (Significantly, *Description of a Struggle*, an early
piece in which something else is attempted, for once, is the
weakest in the book.) And the undeniable success that Kafka
must be granted is of a most curious kind. 'One sheds one's
sicknesses in books—repeats and presents again one's emotions
to be master of them,' wrote D. H. Lawrence, and the sentence
is often quoted nowadays because it gives so succinctly the
fashionable view of the relation between the artist, his work,
and his own disabilities. But no one can say that Kafka ever
'mastered' or 'shed' his sickness in his books, though he certainly
repeated and presented it: presented it, moreover, in what are
recognizable as true works of art, and not mere spewings-forth
of illness. How can one present and analyse illness, weakness,
and disability, without making some attempt to cure them, in
the very act of analysis and presentation? I do not know; I
only know that Kafka managed to do it.

And he did it not only in terms of allegory and fable, but
discursively too, in his notebooks, letters, and aphorisms. The
most acute critic of Kafka is Kafka himself; and again one
wonders how it was possible for him to have so much insight
into his own condition without being able to put it to any
further use. For instance, on the question with which we began,
the relation of Kafka to his fellow-Jews, he could write very
bluntly, 'What have I in common with the Jews, when I have
nothing in common with myself?' And as for the larger question,
Kafka wrote:

> 'As far as I know, I do not have any of the qualities required
> for life, only the common human weakness. With this
> weakness—in this respect it is an enormous strength—I
> took resolutely upon me the negative elements of my epoch,
> which I have not the right to combat, but have the right, so
> to speak, to represent.'

One must concede to him his single 'enormous strength': there
is no one who is better than Kafka at describing, without
shame or pride, all the forms of our imprisonment. There is no

disjunction in his fables between the psychological, the political, and the spiritual—no more than there is in life—and this is one of the reasons for their power; this is one of the evidences of their truth. But in the nature of the case it is not surprising that Kafka's shorter works, like *The Burrow* or *The Metamorphosis*, are much more rewarding than his attempts at full-length novels.

1960

JAMES BALDWIN AND THE
AMERICAN NEGRO

IN HIS FIRST BOOK of essays, *Notes of a Native Son*, James Baldwin can be said to have tried to establish within himself an area of experience which he could feel was truly his own, to do with as he liked; a clearing or a camp-site in which he could enjoy the privacy that any man is entitled to. The peculiar difficulty of the task, as he saw it, arose from the fact that he is an American Negro; and hence the objects of innumerable assumptions and prejudices held about all Negroes (and especially perhaps about Negro writers), irrespective of what they themselves are, individually, or of what they want to be. In that first book Mr Baldwin hacked away desperately at every possible demand or insistence which might be made upon him by his public—'No,' he seemed to be saying continually, 'this isn't me, nor this, nor that, nor this again. I'm a man who doesn't yet know who he is; and it's you, with all your ignorant claims upon me, who prevent me from finding out what I am. And you keep on making these claims upon me, you keep on categorizing me, because you imagine that if you do so, then you'll know better who you are. But I will not become any of the things you want me to be; look how many of your categories I've escaped from already!'

Notes of a Native Son remains, in my opinion, Mr Baldwin's best book, either in fiction or non-fiction: it is more complex and more forceful than any of the others, more inward with the experience it seeks to describe and at the same time more detached from it. But the position at which Mr Baldwin arrived at the end of the book was not one that he himself could linger in. 'Yes,' came the voice of the external world (or was it Mr Baldwin's own? And how can you tell the difference between them?) 'we can see that you are supple enough to escape from all the prisons we had prepared for you. You are not a happy-go-lucky Negro, nor a Marxist Negro; you're not a Faulknerian Negro who is prepared simply to "endure" as long as we call upon you to do so, nor a persecuted, noble Negro whom all right-thinking liberals will find it a pleasure to admire; you're not a *Negritude*-hawking Negro, nor a vengeance-seeking Negro, nor a Negro whose sexual prowess should be an example to us all. You have escaped from us, we grant you. But what have you escaped *to*?'

Mr Baldwin's new collection of essays, *Nobody Knows My Name* is sub-titled 'More Notes of a Native Son'; by intention, and by achievement too, it carries on the argument of the earlier book. Mr Baldwin describes the collection as 'a very small part of a private log-book': in his log-book Mr Baldwin describes the reasons why he returned to the United States from a prolonged exile abroad; he reports on a conference of African writers and artists in Paris; he writes a 'Letter from Harlem' and an article on the riot by American Negroes in the United Nations Assembly, after the death of Patrice Lumumba; two articles come from the Southern States, one being a portrait of a boy who is the only Negro attending an 'integrated' school, in spite of the persecution of his schoolfellows, and the other simply describing Mr Baldwin's own reactions during his visit to the 'Old Country', as he, a New York Negro, calls the South; there is a series of three obituary articles on the Negro novelist, Richard Wright.

From this partial description of the book's contents it is evident that the clearing, the camp-site, to which Mr Baldwin managed to escape has turned out to be, in the end, right in the middle of the American market-place. The private, secret place he was trying to establish for himself has been found among the newspaper headlines and on the country's television screens: it is in the school which is being 'integrated', the restaurant which is being 'sat-in', the gallery of the United Nations building on the Lower East side. To some this might seem a bitter irony, even a confession of defeat. To me, I must confess, it seems nothing of the kind: merely an inevitability, given Mr Baldwin's gifts, his patriotism, the depth to which he cares about his fellow-Negroes and his fellow-Americans. I do not want to make Mr Baldwin's position sound more simple than it really is; but it has quite visibly become a public position, in which he is forced to deal with public issues.

The effects of this on Mr Baldwin's writing are not entirely happy. We hear too often in these essays the voice of his will rather than the voice of his sensibility; there are too many examples of rhetoric, of exhortation, of uplift, of reproach, in the book, and they undoubtedly weaken the impact it makes. But the moral to be drawn from these faults is not at all that writers should eschew the political struggles into which their own inclinations draw them. Anyone who might be inclined to draw that moral should try to imagine what the consequences to his work would have been if Mr Baldwin, feeling as he does, had denied his own deep impulses, and had turned away from the public struggle, in order to protect his 'art'. Life and art make so many different claims, no creative worker can possibly meet them all; every writer has at times to sacrifice the one for the other. But I believe firmly that for any writer his art must follow upon his life; he must live as he most deeply wishes to, and, in an ultimate sense, leave his art to look after itself. If it cannot do so, it will never be much of a growth, anyway.

I am not suggesting that Mr Baldwin's present position is the only possible one for any serious Negro writer to adopt: other writers have different impulses which they must seek to understand and follow. But one cannot possibly say of Mr Baldwin that he should be occupying other, or 'higher', ground: all one can ask, rather, is that he should explore even more thoroughly than he has so far done the ground upon which he is now standing.

Mr Baldwin is an American, and his book is directed so intimately at his fellow-Americans that anyone who is not an American feels himself at a great disadvantage in trying to assess, in a way which would not be superficial, the experiences he has described. In my own case, to speak quite personally, as I must at this point, the difficulty of assessment is perhaps made more acute, rather than less so, by the fact that I was born and brought up in South Africa—a country in which the problem of colour is even more desperate than it is in the United States, but where it assumes such very different forms and shapes. On the other hand, as an ex-South African, and as a Jew, I can claim to know something, both from within and without, of the kind of feeling that is released within groups and individuals when they are threatened, or feel themselves to be threatened, by the demands and prejudices of other groups with whom they share a town, or city, or country. And I know, too, a little of the mythologies and demonologies with which a group in power will attempt to rationalize its own oppressive actions; and of how, in the very processes of oppression, those mythologies may come to have something of the truth in them. How much of the truth ultimately, it is the oppressed who decide: that is the one freedom which cannot be taken from them.

But the cases with which I am familiar are, I repeat, very different from those Mr Baldwin writes about. However, before going on to discuss the greatest difference, and the consequences it seems to have, I should try to indicate the nature of what Mr Baldwin believes to be the experience of the American Negro. That experience, to describe it very briefly, is appalling. It is appalling in the South, where everybody knows it's appalling, not least the white Southerners; but Mr Baldwin insists that it is equally appalling in the North, where everybody imagines that the problem has been 'solved', or at least is being dealt with adequately. Mr Baldwin was horrified by what he saw in the South; but he writes with passion of the 'insults, the indifference and cruelty' which the Northern Negro has to encounter every working day; of the filthy ghettoes in which the Northern Negro is compelled to live; of the rackets which exploit for gain his poverty and powerlessness; of the delinquency, the drug-addiction, and the ignorance which continue to generate themselves in ever more brutal forms among these insulted and injured people. I should say, too, that Mr Baldwin writes with only occasional lapses into histrionics; rather, with an evident attempt to avoid self-pity, and to be restrained and charitable towards both white and black Americans. Yet his summing-up is this: 'Negroes are . . . ignored in the North and are under surveillance in the South and suffer hideously in both places.'

There is, moreover, one peculiarly American aspect of the suffering of Negroes which Mr Baldwin brings most sharply into focus. Is it really worse to be oppressed by a power which says, in effect, 'Yes, I am an oppressor, I'm filled with hatred towards you and acknowledge my hate as the only link between us'—is it worse to be oppressed by such a power than by one which speaks and has spoken for hundreds of years of liberty and the pursuit of happiness; which asserts daily through the mouths of its schoolchildren that it is 'one nation, indivisible, under God, with liberty and justice for all'; which offers you posts in the Cabinet and a chance for the Presidency in a generation's time; and which, when you then step forward merely to send your child to a decent school or to stand in line for a cup of coffee or to buy a house in a middle-class suburb, attacks you and your children with bricks and spittle, abuse and truncheons?

South Africa is mentioned several times in Mr Baldwin's book, and always as the worst place of all, the last term of comparison he can invoke to suggest the intensity of Negro suffering in America. Now it is certain that conditions in South Africa are thoroughly bad; and that more and more intense hatred and anger accumulate every day among the country's oppressed blacks. Yet it remains true, too, that the most cheerful people one sees in the streets of South Africa today are the black people. I have been met with blank incredulity when I have said this in conversation with people in England; but it is true, and I am not the only South African, black or white, who has seen it. And it is true for a number of reasons, only one of which we need go into here—which is that the blacks are the majority within South Africa itself, and overwhelmingly so within the entire continent. They know that, eventually, and no matter how long their present tribulations may last, they cannot lose the struggle in which they have found themselves. Though the thought has yet to make its way, consciously, into the minds of millions of Africans, even the least conscious among them knows already that one day they will have power.

Power: the ugly word is out. In nothing is Mr Baldwin more of an American, and more of an American Negro, than the reluctance with which he discusses questions of power. Reluctance may seem an odd word to use about someone who at a certain point writes of himself: 'Well, I know how power works, it has worked on me, and if I didn't know how power worked, I would be dead.' But Mr Baldwin makes my case, indirectly, when he goes on to say, 'I have simply never been able to afford myself any illusions concerning the manipulation of that power.' For what he is confessing here is that for a Negro the exercise of direct political and economic power appears to be all but unattainable. And it is at this very point, I feel, that the weaknesses of Mr Baldwin's writing tend to reveal themselves. Instead of analysing the consequences of Negro powerlessness, or speculating about the kinds of power they may hope to win for themselves, he too frequently contents himself with making moral appeals, or with issuing warnings. The warnings, God knows, are justified; the appeals are indeed those of reason and intelligence and compassion. But does he believe they will be listened to? Does he *really* believe it? And if they are not listened to, what does he propose to do then, what other courses of action does he believe to be open to him?

The American Negro, Mr Baldwin believes, tells the white Americans 'where the bottom is: *because he is there*, and *where* he is, beneath us, we know where the limits are and how far we must not fall. We must not fall beneath him.' There is only one way a group can rise from such a position: through the exercise of power. And Mr Baldwin all but explicitly admits as much in his repeated references to the effect upon American Negroes of the emergence of the independent black states of Africa; when he writes, for example, 'The American Negro can no longer, nor will he ever again, be controlled by the white American's image of him. This fact has everything to do with the rise of Africa in world affairs,' or again,

'The power of the white world to control (the Negroes') identities was crumbling as they were born; and by the time they were able to react to the world, Africa was on the stage of history. This could not but have an extraordinary effect on their own morale. . . . It also signals, at last, the end of the Negro situation in this country, as we have so far known it. Any effort, from here on out, to keep the Negro in his "place" can only have the most extreme and unlucky repercussions.'

What I am asking for, I suppose, is that Mr Baldwin should tell us what he imagines those 'extreme and unlucky repercussions' might be, within himself and among American Negroes—leaving aside, for the moment, what they may be among the coloured nations of the world. This is not a small thing to ask; for what it presupposes is that, having so little effective power locally, the militant American Negroes, for all the determination and self-restraint they have so far shown, may yet fail to achieve their ends, and that Mr Baldwin's hopes for 'a country in which there are no minorities—for the first time in the history of the world' may remain illusory.

It is profoundly to be hoped, for every conceivable reason, that the American Negroes will be able to win for themselves a place other than the one they now occupy; but the fate of all easily identifiable and powerless minorities in the past does not allow one to nourish any large and easy expectations—even though the United States is 'different'; even though the country is goaded forward, and not merely tormented, by the high ideals it has explicitly formulated for itself. The irony of the situation, however, is that the answers Mr Baldwin could bring from his present positon may prove very useful, one day, to the rest of us: to the whites all over the world, who are slowly, reluctantly, incredulously beginning to realize that they are a minority, too, in a world that they no longer own.

However, the burden of further self-scrutiny does not rest upon Mr Baldwin alone, for the effect of reading his book must be to make anyone who thinks of himself as a liberal reflect more deeply upon the nature and the conditions of his own liberalism. I do not mean here, only, that he is forced to look for the prejudices, irrationalities and compulsions which might lie hidden among his own habits of thought; but also that he is forced to examine again the extent to which he really believes that it is possible to moderate and ameliorate the operations of brute power in human affairs.

To deal with the question of prejudice first; with the mythologies and demonologies which Mr Baldwin analyses in these essays, as he did in his earlier book. He points out again and again how the Negro 'is penalized for the guilty imagination of the white people who invest him with their hates and longings', and how he becomes 'the principal target of their sexual paranoia'. In this book, as in *Notes of a Native Son*, he traces the origins of these paranoias to the first shocked confrontation between the Puritan white and the tribal African, and to the exploitations and guilts of the colonial and slave-owning periods, to which that first confrontation so rapidly led. And again and again, as anyone brought up in a society racked with prejudice against the blacks would have to, I found myself agreeing with him: yes, it was so; yes, I had seen these compulsions betrayed in words and actions; yes, I had even tried to write about them, in words similar to Mr Baldwin's own. Yet it would be less than honest if I weren't to admit that I found myself offering these agreements, almost invariably, *on behalf of others*, not on my own behalf. And I imagine that something similar would be the reaction of many of the whites who will read Mr Baldwin's book—or, for that matter, this article.

Mr Baldwin would possibly regard this as no more than a further example of the liberal complacency and self-righteousness he so often inveighs against; but, with the example of what is happening in Africa so vividly in my mind, I cannot help feeling a certain dissatisfaction, even an impatience, with the methods of analysis he uses and I have used in the past; I cannot help wondering how relevant or useful they still are. I have suggested that the great, perhaps the insuperable, problem which faces the American Negroes in their struggle is their present lack of political and economic power in American society. The world respects those who have power, and abuses, maltreats, or patronizes those who have none; and the abuse, maltreatment and patronage assume every possible form which general tradition and individual malevolence, ignorance and insensitivity may suggest. Almost, it seems a kind of flattery of the oppressor to say more of him than this; or at least to permit him to imagine that his fantasies and rationalizations would be of any importance at all, were it not for his power.

When I speak of 'the world' in this way, I do not exclude those who think of themselves as liberals; I do not exclude myself. I know from my own experience that the opportunity of meeting, outside South Africa, black politicians and intellectuals who have won some direct power for themselves, and who are already able to take the exercise of that power for granted, has had a greatly liberating effect upon me: more than anything else, these meetings have enabled me to cast from myself a part of that burden of pity and anxiety, guilt and automatic benevolence towards people with black skins which my South African experience had imposed upon me. This is not to say that such meetings between whites and blacks are without pains, on both sides; but they are pains of a different kind from those of which Mr Baldwin writes.

Thus I have no wish to defend the characteristic and traditional postures of white liberalism; they are, in their own way, cramped, bullying and dishonest. I realize that there are many 'liberals' who are still unable to perceive that it is, for example, as grotesque and baneful to admire the Negro because of the sexuality you impute to him as it is to hate him for the same reason. Yet, under the new circumstances obtaining in the world today, I don't believe that it is an impossibly difficult task to school oneself out of follies of that kind, if the opportunity is given to one, and if one really wishes to do so. Nor, in spite of Mr Baldwin's insistence to the contrary, do I believe it impossible for a white man to have any conception of the inwardness of Negro experience: it depends on who the Negro is, and who the white man, and in what way they meet.

However, if one thinks of the world as invariably making responses of a more or less respectful nature to the facts of power, and if one sees in oneself something of these same responses; if one thinks of history as simply an ebb and flow of power, always producing in those who possess it the same impulses towards the maltreatment or patronage of those who plainly do not possess it, what point is there in asking the white man, whether in Alabama or South Africa, to refrain from abusing his power? Or in hoping that the black man, in his turn, will not abuse the power he is so swiftly winning for himself in other parts of the world?

The questions suggest their own dispirited answers: that is why, perhaps, liberals like myself have taken to asking them so frequently these days. For the fact is that 'history' and 'the world' alike show that it is indeed possible, at certain times, and in certain places, to moderate the operation of brute power; just as it is possible to struggle with one's own responses to these operations. The questions to be asked, rather, in each case, is whether we have such a place here, whether this is the time, and what alternative powers of principle, persuasion and example it may be possible effectively to use.

Whether or not the United States is a place where persuasion and example can undo the injustices of which Mr Baldwin speaks we shall know within a matter of years. It is certain that only years, not generations, are left in which the injustices can be undone. The movement of our time being what it is, it is suicidal for white Americans to harry and persecute black men because they are black—as suicidal, and almost as directly so, as it is for white South Africans.

1961